THE
HISTORY
OF
ISSUES

Immigration

THE
HISTORY
OF
ISSUES

Immigration

Laura K. Egendorf, *Book Editor*

Bruce Glassman, *Vice President*
Bonnie Szumski, *Publisher*
Helen Cothran, *Managing Editor*

GREENHAVEN PRESS
An imprint of Thomson Gale, a part of The Thomson Corporation

THOMSON

GALE

Detroit • New York • San Francisco • San Diego • New Haven, Conn.
Waterville, Maine • London • Munich

LIBRARY OF CONGRESS CATALOGING-IN-PUBLICATION DATA

Immigration / Laura K. Egendorf, book editor.
  p. cm. — (The history of issues)
Includes bibliographical references and index.
ISBN 0-7377-2871-X (lib. : alk. paper)
  1. United States—Emigration and immigration—History. 2. United States—Emigration and immigration—Government policy—History. I. Egendorf, Laura K., 1973– . II. Series.
JV6450.I558 2006
304.8'73—dc22   2005046156

Contents

tion are exaggerating the number of immigrants flooding into the country.

and Effective Death Penalty Act in 1996 resulted in the unfair detention and deportation of thousands of illegal immigrants.

In the 1940s, at the height of the Holocaust, Jews struggled to create a nation of their own in Palestine, a region of the Middle East that at the time was controlled by Britain. The British had placed limits on Jewish immigration to Palestine, hampering efforts to provide refuge to Jews fleeing the Holocaust. In response to this and other British policies, an underground Jewish resistance group called Irgun began carrying out terrorist attacks against British targets in Palestine, including immigration, intelligence, and police offices. Most famously, the group bombed the King David Hotel in Jerusalem, the site of a British military headquarters. Although the British were warned well in advance of the attack, they failed to evacuate the building. As a result, ninety-one people were killed (including fifteen Jews) and forty-five were injured.

Early in the twentieth century, Ireland, which had long been under British rule, was split into two countries. The south, populated mostly by Catholics, eventually achieved independence and became the Republic of Ireland. Northern Ireland, mostly Protestant, remained under British control. Catholics in both the north and south opposed British control of the north, and the Irish Republican Army (IRA) sought unification of Ireland as an independent nation. In 1969, the IRA split into two factions. A new radical wing, the Provisional IRA, was created and soon undertook numerous terrorist bombings and killings throughout Northern Ireland, the Republic of Ireland, and even in England. One of its most notorious attacks was the 1974 bombing of a Birmingham, England, bar that killed nineteen people.

In the mid-1990s, an Islamic terrorist group called al Qaeda began carrying out terrorist attacks against American targets overseas. In communications to the media, the organization listed several complaints against the United States. It generally opposed all U.S. involvement and presence in the Middle East. It particularly objected to the presence of U.S. troops in Saudi Arabia, which is the home of several Islamic holy sites. And it strongly condemned the United States for supporting the nation of Israel, which it claimed was an oppressor of Muslims. In 1998 al Qaeda's leaders issued a fatwa (a religious legal statement) calling for Muslims to kill Americans. Al Qaeda acted on this order many times—most memorably on September 11, 2001, when it attacked the World Trade Center and the Pentagon, killing nearly three thousand people.

These three groups—Irgun, the Provisional IRA, and al Qaeda—have achieved varied results. Irgun's terror campaign contributed to Britain's decision to pull out of Palestine and to support the creation of Israel in 1948. The Provisional IRA's tactics kept pressure on the British, but they also alienated many would-be supporters of independence for Northern Ireland. Al Qaeda's attacks provoked a strong U.S. military response but did not lessen America's involvement in the Middle East nor weaken its support of Israel. Despite these different results, the means and goals of these groups were similar. Although they emerged in different parts of the world during different eras and in support of different causes, all three had one thing in common: They all used clandestine violence to undermine a government they deemed oppressive or illegitimate.

The destruction of oppressive governments is not the only goal of terrorism. For example, terror is also used to minimize dissent in totalitarian regimes and to promote extreme ideologies. However, throughout history the motivations of terrorists have been remarkably similar, proving the old adage that "the more things change, the more they remain the same." Arguments for and against terrorism thus boil down to the same set of universal arguments regardless of the age: Some argue that terrorism is justified to change (or, in the case of state terror, to maintain) the prevailing political order; others respond that terrorism is inhumane and unacceptable under any circumstances. These basic views transcend time and place.

Similar fundamental arguments apply to other controversial social issues. For instance, arguments over the death penalty have always featured competing views of justice. Scholars cite biblical texts to claim that a person who takes a life must forfeit his or her life, while others cite religious doctrine to support their view that only God can take a human life. These arguments have remained essentially the same throughout the centuries. Likewise, the debate over euthanasia has persisted throughout the history of Western civilization. Supporters argue that it is compassionate to end the suffering of the dying by hastening their impending death; opponents insist that it is society's duty to make the dying as comfortable as possible as death takes its natural course.

Greenhaven Press's The History of Issues series illustrates this constancy of arguments surrounding major social issues. Each volume in the series focuses on one issue—including terrorism, the death penalty, and euthanasia—and examines how the debates have both evolved and remained essentially the same over the years. Primary documents such as newspaper articles, speeches, and government reports illuminate historical developments and offer perspectives from throughout history. Secondary sources provide overviews and commentaries from a more contemporary perspective. An introduction begins each anthology and supplies essential context and background. An annotated table of contents, chronology, and index allow for easy reference, and a bibliography and list of organizations to contact point to additional sources of information on the book's topic. With these features, The History of Issues series permits readers to glimpse both the historical and contemporary dimensions of humanity's most pressing and controversial social issues.

Introduction

The immigration of millions of people to the United States has shaped the development of the country. Immigrants have brought energy, hard work, and new ideas to the United States for several hundred years. However, opponents of immigration contend that instead of improving the quality of American life, immigrants threaten it by spreading foreign viruses, committing crimes, and refusing to wholly adopt the dominant American rituals. One of the most enduring arguments against immigration developed in the 1830s, not long after the first major wave of immigrants into the United States began arriving. Known as nativism, this opposition to immigration emerged because its mainly Protestant, northern European proponents wanted to protect their culture from immigrants who practiced alien religions and had different customs and beliefs. Initially, nativists opposed the immigration of the Irish. In subsequent generations, anti-immigrant groups have resisted the immigration of Jews, Asians, Mexicans, and Arabs— among other populations. While nativists have opposed various immigrant groups for more than 150 years, their fear of foreign influence has remained constant.

Irish Immigration: Unwelcome Catholics

Even before the colonies declared their independence, many of the colonists were intolerant of immigrants who were not Protestants. Prejudice against Catholic immigrants can be traced as far back as the mid-eighteenth century. For example, historian Timothy W. Bosworth writes in the *Catholic Historical Review* that in the 1750s, Maryland law allowed for children to be removed from Catholic homes and raised in Protestant families where they could learn traditional Anglican values. Nonetheless, it was not until an influx of Irish immigrants began to arrive in the nineteenth century that American nativism became a strong movement.

The first major wave of Irish immigration began in 1830. Approximately 350,000 Irish immigrants arrived between 1830 and 1845; the Irish potato famine of the late 1840s caused many more Irish to leave their country, pushing that total to nearly 1 million. During this period, Irish immigrants comprised close to one-half of America's foreign population. The arrival of so many largely Catholic Irish immigrants was resented by many native-born Americans, who were pre-dominantly Protestant. Nearly one hundred years after the situation described by Bosworth, conflicts between Protes-tants and Catholics over the education of Catholic children still persisted throughout the eastern states. Historian Kevin Kenny describes one such conflict in his book *The American Irish: A History*. He states that in New York City in the 1830s, Irish immigrants, uncomfortable with the Protes-tant domination of the public school system, established parochial schools for their children. This action upset Protestant nativists who felt that by rejecting American public schools, Irish Catholics were showing that they had little interest in assimilation. Kenny writes, "Why, the na-tivists wanted to know, were public schools not good enough for Irish immigrants? This question, among others, lay behind the great anti-Catholic riots that broke out in Philadelphia and its suburb, Kensington, in 1844."[1]

As Kenny's comments suggest, New York City was not the only site of tension between Protestants and Catholics. Two months after the Kensington riots, more violence took place in Philadelphia when native-born Protestants, angry not only with the disagreements over schooling but also with falling wages (for which they blamed immigrants), in-vaded the Catholic sections of the suburbs. The rioters burned down two churches and set a third aflame. Battles between the nativist mobs and Irish workers lasted for four days, leaving nine people dead and twenty wounded.

The Catholic immigrants' religious practices also outraged some Protestant nativists. In the eyes of Protestants, Catholics' use of such objects as rosaries and holy water was akin to the practice of magic. In addition, the Catholic belief that the wine and wafers used in the communion ceremony were the actual blood and body of Christ, and not just symbols, struck Protestants as overly superstitious. The general distrust Protestants had for Catholic ritual was amplified by Maria Monk's book *Awful Disclosures*, published in 1836. Although her stories were eventually proved to be a hoax, Monk's description of the horrors she saw at a nunnery, including infanticide and sexual relations between priests and nuns, further darkened some Protestants' view of Catholics.

Although many nativists distrusted Irish immigrants and opposed their settlement in the United States, their anti-immigrant movement did not have much political power until a group of native-born Americans formed the Know-Nothing Party in 1849. Officially known as the "American Party," the Know-Nothing Party received its nickname because it had originally developed out of a secret society whose members vowed that they would deny any knowledge of the society, a nativist organization called the Order of the Star Spangled Banner. Its members staunchly opposed immigration and particularly Catholic immigrants. Not surprisingly, the party was strongest in areas where Irish populations were largest, such as Massachusetts. In 1854 the party dominated Massachusetts's state elections, winning the governor's office, the state senate, and most of the seats in the state house of representatives. In addition more than one hundred U.S. congressmen in the mid-1850s were members of the Know-Nothing Party. Their power was short-lived, however, ending with intraparty conflict over slavery.

Life for Irish immigrants started to improve after the Civil War. Although Protestants and Catholics still had serious conflicts—the most violent of which were the Orange and Green Riots of 1870–71, in which more than sixty people died in New York City—the Irish had gradually begun to build more stable and prosperous lives in their new country. "The famine generation of Irish immigrants," Kenny notes, "had established a foothold in the United States." However, he points out, "their social position was still precarious, with 40 per cent working as labourers, and anti-Irish racism and nativism far from dissipated."[2]

Despite the struggles the Irish faced in America, they eventually began to gain the acceptance of native-born Americans. The bravery displayed by the Irish American soldiers on both sides of the Civil War helped improve public opinion toward Irish immigrants. Businesses that had previously refused to hire Irish Americans became more welcoming, enabling many of these immigrants to thrive in the railroad and construction industries—industries that were key as the nation continued to expand westward. The growing economic power of Irish Americans was accompanied by increasing political strength. The sizable Irish population in major cities such as Boston and New York afforded them great influence at the polls. By the 1880s both cities had Irish-American mayors. The Irish-American political machines, which provided crucial social services while ensuring voter loyalty, retained their strength well into the twentieth century.

Jewish Immigration

Nativism did not end once Irish immigrants began to be more accepted by the greater American society. The next target for nativist animus was the European Jews who began arriving in the middle-to-late nineteenth century and early twentieth century. Like the Irish Catholics, the Jews were viewed with suspicion because of their religion and unfamiliar practices.

The German Jews who began arriving in the 1840s were quick to assimilate, learning English as soon as they could

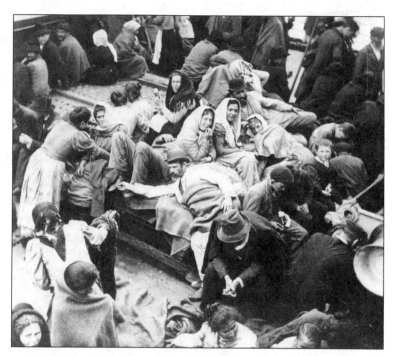
European immigrants endured a long Atlantic crossing in hopes of starting a new, prosperous life in America.

and shedding traditional Jewish garb, religious practices, and dietary beliefs with the aim of making themselves secular Americans. For the eastern European and Russian Jews who started to reach American shores in the 1870s, adapting to the United States was much more difficult, as they were typically poorer and more unskilled than the German Jews and thus found it more difficult to establish an economic foothold. Abraham J. Karp writes in the introduction to his book *Golden Door to America: The Jewish Immigrant Experience*, "It was only in comparison to conditions in eastern Europe that America was considered home and haven. In truth, Jews were beset here by economic discrimination, social exclusion, and a pervasive anti-Semitism usually genteel but on occasion overt and blatant."[3]

Like the Irish Catholics, Jewish immigrants were also

viewed with suspicion by mainstream Christian America, and anti-Semitism was part of the public school curriculum. For example, many schools used the popular *McGuffey's Readers*, which, according to writer Elliott Abrams, "characterized the Jews of Roman times as living in 'the most licentious fanaticism' and expressed continuing contempt for Jews and their religion."[4] Jews were also violently attacked and harassed by their new neighbors, with East Coast peddlers suffering much of the abuse.

Working class Jews were not the only Jews to experience discrimination. History professor and author John Higham contends that Jewish immigrants at the higher levels of society also faced anti-Jewish sentiment. According to Higham,

> Discrimination developed where and when Jews participated heavily in a general middle class scramble for prestige; it developed where and when a hectic pace of social climbing made the guardians of distinction afraid of being "invaded." It grew in eastern summer resorts, fraternities, and urban real estate offices, not just in the South and the West where farmers were beginning to murmur about the shadowy power of the International Jew.[5]

Some writers cast doubts about whether Jewish immigrants were as ill-treated as Karp and Abrams describe. Ironically, in at least one instance these writers' denials of harsh discrimination against Jews ironically reveal their own anti-Semitism. Such a view can be found in an August 1891 article in *North American Review*, in which Godwin Smith castigates the "marked and repellent nationality" of Jews and asserts that they should have little to complain about. Using the traditional anti-Semitic canards that Jews control America's wealth and media, Smith writes, "The Jew of America and western Europe has not much reason to complain of his present position. In a society of which wealth is the ruling power, his financial skill, sharpened by immemorial practice and aided by the confederacy of his kinsmen, makes him the master of wealth."[6]

Discrimination against Jews remained strong into the 1940s, with quotas limiting their entrance into private clubs, universities, and certain occupations, such as banking, law, and insurance. After World War II, the Holocaust finally made hatred of Jews less acceptable in the United States. Nativism also began to decline as Jewish Americans, like the Irish who had come before them, developed more political power.

Asian Immigrants

Nativists initially targeted certain European immigrants but in the nineteenth century focused their anti-immigration efforts on immigrants who began arriving from Asia, primarily China and Japan. Like the Irish immigrants of the early nineteenth century, who helped build the canals that made it easier for Americans to travel and trade, Chinese immigrants helped strengthen America's infrastructure by constructing railroads in the west. The Chinese also labored in western mines, arriving in California soon after the start of the Gold Rush in the 1850s, where they were blamed by native miners for driving down wages—just as Irish workers had been accused of doing on the East Coast. Ironically, despite these similarities and their history of discrimination, Irish Americans were staunchly opposed to Chinese immigration. As Kenny writes, "The hostility of Irish workers to the Chinese was arguably the most intense of all."[7] According to Kenny, Irish Americans believed that their dislike for Chinese immigrants proved that they deserved to be part of mainstream white America. However, the Irish Americans were not the only group of nativists to discriminate against and even attack Chinese immigrants; throughout the 1880s, violent mobs throughout the western United States forced Chinese immigrants out of their homes and businesses.

Even when the economy improved at the turn of the twentieth century, attitudes toward Asian immigrants did not improve. Discrimination occurred in San Francisco, where the children of Chinese and Japanese immigrants were required to attend segregated schools. Asian immigrants continued to face economic problems, especially in California, where Asian farmers were often driven off their farmland by white farmers. In 1913 the California Alien Land Law was enacted, barring Japanese and East Indians from owning land. Asian immigrants were also frequently attacked by anti-immigration mobs.

In such an atmosphere, it is not surprising that several of the earliest laws restricting immigration targeted Asians. The first such law was the Exclusion Act of 1882, which barred the entrance of Chinese immigrants for ten years. The act was renewed several times before being overturned in 1943 and replaced by a quota. The Gentleman's Agreement of 1907 barred most Japanese immigration for the next ten years, while the Immigration Act of 1917 prohibited all Asian immigration, with the exception of entrants from Japan and the Philippines. The worst government act affecting Asian immigrants took place during World War II. Approximately 120,000 Japanese immigrants and native-born Japanese Americans were placed in internment camps in western states because the government feared they might be loyal to the Axis Japanese government.

The Debate over Mexican Immigrants

Nativism seemed to weaken after World War II, when the U.S. government began to loosen immigration laws in order to ease the entrance of war refugees. In 1965 Congress passed the Immigration Act, ending forty years of immigration quotas based on the country of origin. Instead, the act established an annual limit of 170,000 immigrants from the Eastern Hemisphere and 120,000 immigrants from the Western Hemisphere. However, by increasing the number of immigrants who could enter the United States, the law helped usher in a new era of nativism.

Debate over immigration from Mexico was largely nonexistent before the 1930s. In fact, the immigration of Mexican

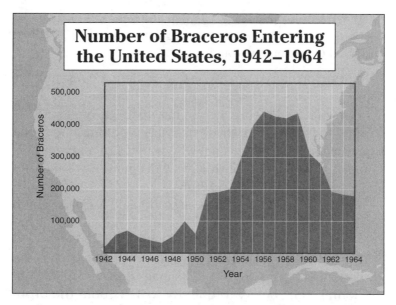

Number of Braceros Entering the United States, 1942–1964

workers was even encouraged as part of the bracero, or guest worker, program that ran from 1942 to 1964. The program was created to allow Mexicans to legally cross the border in order to replace the manual laborers who enlisted during World War II. After the program ended, however, the question of Mexican immigration became a serious domestic policy issue, especially in states such as California and Arizona, where legal and illegal immigration from south of the border became a frequently debated topic.

Present-day nativists contend that the greatest threat to American culture comes from the influx of Hispanic immigrants, both legal and illegal. Political scientist Samuel P. Huntington opines in an article from *Foreign Policy* that if Mexican immigration were to end, the United States would benefit in several ways. He writes,

> The impact of Mexican immigration on the United States becomes evident when one imagines what would happen if Mexican immigration abruptly stopped. The annual flow of legal immigrants would drop by about 175,000. . . . Illegal entries would diminish dramatically. The wages of low-income U.S. citizens would improve.

Debates over the use of Spanish and whether English should be made the official language of state and national governments would subside.[8]

Huntington goes on to argue that white male resentment over losing jobs to Hispanics and other immigrants could lead to what he labels a "white nativism" movement. According to Huntington, these nativists would not be racial supremacists but rather men who want to preserve American culture in the face of what they deem Mexico's morally and intellectually inferior culture.

Several organizations have also opposed Mexican immigration. Although they may not identify themselves as nativists, groups such as the John Birch Society and the Federation for American Immigration Reform (FAIR) share views similar to Huntington. In its magazine *New American*, the John Birch Society frequently writes about the problems that could occur if the United States makes it easier for Mexicans to immigrate. The society and FAIR are among the opponents of President George W. Bush's proposal to offer amnesty to illegal immigrants. In his article "Bush's Coming Amnesty Plan," *New American* writer William F. Jasper maintains that allowing more Mexicans to enter America is a reckless idea. He cites immigration experts who argue that a previous effort at amnesty, created under the 1986 Immigration Reform and Control Act, failed to control American borders, and that implementing a new amnesty program would be costly and ineffective. Such a program, according to Jasper and his fellow analysts, would not only be expensive but would also make it easier for immigrants who pose a threat to national security to enter the United States.

Anti-Muslim and Arab Nativism

While opposition to immigration prior to the twentieth century mainly centered on the economic and cultural impact that foreigners might have on the United States, after September 2001, some critics of immigration began to argue that immigrants could be a threat to the safety and security of Americans. The terrorist attacks of September 11, 2001, were the work of Middle Eastern Muslim extremists who had entered America with the purpose of planning the hijackings that killed over three thousand people.

As with nativism toward earlier groups, anti-immigration attitudes toward Muslim immigrants is based heavily on a distrust of foreign culture. Anti-immigration commentators charged that the acts committed by the terrorists are proof that Muslim extremism has found a foothold in the United States. They point to the use of anti-American texts in mosques and Islamic schools as an indication that hatred of American values such as tolerance and democracy, coupled with a call for jihad (holy war), is being inculcated in Muslim children, raising the possibility of future acts of terrorism. In their view, allowing people to emigrate from traditionally Muslim Middle Eastern countries, or not doing enough to prevent illegal immigration from those nations, will only make it easier for Muslim extremists to spread their anti-American views.

While many people, including President Bush, argued in the wake of September 11 that the vast majority of Muslims in the United States and throughout the world are repulsed by acts of terrorism, some critics of immigration have charged that Muslim Americans and immigrants present a threat that cannot be ignored. Daniel Pipes, a prominent writer on the Middle East and Islam, contends that the United States must increase its scrutiny of Muslim Americans because of the danger they represent to national security. He writes in the *New York Post* in January 2003,

> There is no escaping the unfortunate fact that Muslim government employees in law enforcement, the military and the diplomatic corps need to be watched for connections to terrorism, as do Muslim chaplains in prisons and the armed forces. Muslim visitors and immigrants must undergo additional background checks. Mosques require a scrutiny beyond that applied to churches and temples.[9]

The Legacy of Nativism

Nativist attitudes toward immigrants have existed in the United States for more than 150 years and will likely continue to do so. A 2004 poll conducted by National Public Radio, the Kaiser Family Foundation, and Harvard University's Kennedy School of Government found that Americans have mixed feelings about immigration. Forty-one percent of Americans polled believe legal immigration should be decreased, while another 37 percent say that it should stay at its current level. Thirty percent of the respondents believe immigration has been good for America, while 39 percent disagree. Native-born Americans also believe strongly, by a 62 percent to 39 percent margin (figures were rounded off), that immigrants should adopt basic American cultures and values.

However, despite the strong, and often negative, opinions many Americans have about immigration and the means used by opponents of immigration to discourage foreigners from entering the United States, some Americans continue to support immigration. One of their major arguments is that immigration remains a significant source of population growth, which is important in a country with a declining birth rate. In fact, American immigrants throughout history have found support from many of their new neighbors. Nativist writings have long been countered by Americans who laud the contribution of the nation's foreign-born citizenry. Such sentiments are typified by Daniel T. Griswold, an associate director at the Cato Institute. He declares in the magazine *Insight on the News* that immigrants are not an economic threat to American workers and argues, "We are a nation of immigrants. Successive waves of immigrants have kept our country demographically young, enriched our culture and added to our productive capacity as a nation, enhancing our influence in the world."[10] The perhaps endless debate between proponents and opponents of immigration is addressed by the authors in *History of Issues: Immigration*. They consider the potential threat of immigration, quotas and other policies that limit legal immigration, and how best to control illegal immigration.

Notes

1. Kevin Kenny, *The American Irish: A History*. New York: Pearson Education Limited, 2000, p. 78.
2. Kenny, *The American Irish: A History*, p. 129.
3. Abraham J. Karp, ed., *Golden Door to America: The Jewish Immigrant Experience*. New York: Viking Press, 1976, p. 15.
4. Elliott Abrams, "Anti-Semitism in America," *National Review*, May 30, 1994.
5. John Higham, "Another Look at Nativism," *Catholic Historical Review*, July 1958.
6. Godwin Smith, excerpt from an article in *North American Review*, August 1891. Republished in Karp, ed., *Golden Door to America*, p. 99.
7. Kenny, *The American Irish: A History*, p. 157.
8. Samuel P. Huntington, "The Hispanic Challenge," *Foreign Policy*, March/April 2004.
9. Daniel Pipes, "The Enemy Within," *New York Post*, January 24, 2003.
10. Daniel T. Griswold, "Immigrants Have Enriched American Culture and Enhanced Our Influence in the World," *Insight on the News*, February 18, 2002.

THE
HISTORY
OF
ISSUES

CHAPTER 1

Debating the Threat of Immigration

Chapter Preface

Few groups of people are as feared as immigrants. As strangers to a nation, they are frequently viewed as threats to the job prospects, wealth, and security of native-born citizens. One area of particular concern to natives is the health risks that immigrants could pose. In addition to their culture, foreigners can bring with them virulent diseases. Two health scares more than a century apart show how the threat of disease is an ongoing issue central to immigration debates.

The cholera epidemic of the 1890s led to changes in U.S. immigration policies. Cholera is an infectious disease caused by bacteria found in fecal-contaminated food and water. A strain known as Asiatic cholera began in India in 1881 and spread throughout the rest of the world over the next fifteen years. Eastern Europe was particularly affected—more than 300,000 Russians died of cholera. The epidemic reached the United States in the fall of 1892, which perhaps not coincidentally was a record year for immigration. The result, as Alan M. Kraus observes in his book, *Silent Travelers: Germs, Genes, and the "Immigrant Menace,"* was "an increase in federal public health responsibilities, especially with respect to the potential health menace posed by immigration." In an effort to control the epidemic, eastern European immigrants who had traveled in steerage were removed from incoming ships and put under a twenty-day quarantine. The quarantine lasted from September 1892 until January 1893. Once the cholera plague had been eradicated in the United States, eastern European immigration began to return to its earlier levels. However, the government still feared future outbreaks. In 1893 Congress passed the Rayner-Harris National Quarantine Act, which allowed the president to suspend immigration on a temporary basis and established procedures with which to study the medical condition of immigrants.

More than a century later, immigrants are again being linked with an epidemic. This time the disease is tuberculosis. Although the number of tuberculosis cases in the United States has been largely declining since the 1950s, a disproportionate number of today's cases come from immigrants born in Mexico, Vietnam, and the Philippines, raising concerns that these foreign-born populations could cause a new TB outbreak. Columnist Samuel Francis points out that a report issued by the Centers of Disease Control in 2000 "showed that the six states with the highest incidence of [tuberculosis] were the same as those to which most immigrants flock: California, New York, Texas, Florida, New Jersey, and Illinois." Statistics from the CDC revealed that 15,874 Americans were diagnosed with TB in 2003, with 7,902 of the affected being foreign-born. Of that subset, 2,024 were Mexican-born, 912 were from the Philippines, and 663 were natives of Vietnam. According to the *Toronto Star*, Canada is experiencing a similar problem: Ninety percent of Torontonians with TB are immigrants or refugees. Francis suggests that because legal immigrants and refugees are screened for tuberculosis, the threat is largely from illegal immigration. He argues that in order to ensure the safety of Americans, it may be necessary to deport illegal immigrants.

For nearly two centuries immigrants have been viewed with both warmth and fear by Americans. While their contribution to American society has been positive in many ways, the fears over immigrant-caused epidemics shows that foreign-born Americans will likely continue to be viewed as possible threats. The authors in this chapter consider whether immigrants are a threat to the United States or if those concerns are unfounded.

Irish Immigrants Are a Threat to American Politics

SAMUEL C. BUSEY

Prejudice against Irish immigrants was widespread in the United States during the nineteenth century. These immigrants, who were largely Catholic, were viewed as threats by Americans, most of whom were Protestants. Many Americans were worried that Irish Americans were garnering too much political power. One of the people who expressed these concerns was Samuel C. Busey. In the following selection, excerpted from his 1856 book Immigration: Its Evils and Consequences, *he argues that Irish immigrants have been a political threat since 1814. According to Busey, Irish Catholic voters in both Ireland and America have demonstrated their willingness to use violence, intimidation, and propaganda to get their candidates elected, even when it means the defeat of better qualified men. Busey was a doctor at Georgetown University and the author of several books.*

[F]oreign] organizations have not stopped with a mere enumeration of their principles. They have boldly entered the political arena, asserted their right to share with us in legislation and with a zeal and determination worthy of a better cause, sought to engraft upon our institutions the "principles which they imbibed in early youth." The abjuration of their allegiance to the country of their birth has

---

Samuel C. Busey, *Immigration: Its Evils and Consequences*. New York: De Witt & Davenport, 1856.

not divested them of their principles.

The oath of allegiance to ours, has not infused into them the spirit of our government. They have left home and kindred, severed associations, and cut asunder the ties of relationship, but the principles they "imbibed in youth," still cling to them. They have brought with them the "maxims of absolute monarchies," or exchanged them "for an unbounded licentiousness.". . .

A Longtime Threat

As early as 1814 the Irish were troublesome to our people, and were not unfrequently denounced as such by the press of those days. A friend has handed the author a copy of the "Herald of Liberty," published at Augusta, Maine, bearing date April 30th, 1814, speaking of the envoys sent to Gottenburg, to negotiate peace with Great Britain; it says in a letter from Washington of April 12th,

> Whenever any measure displeases these licensed calumniators, they are as insolent and vituperous against government as they are mean and fawning when they are pleased. It is known to Mr. Madison, who has American feeling, that at a late meeting of the Tammany Savage society in New York, a motion was made to denounce him, a la mode de Robespierre,[1] for his message to Congress for the repeal of the embargo law,[2] and that it was negatived only by a small majority. This society is principally made up of the feces of the sewers of Ireland, & I am confident the President would consent to the introduction of any article in a treaty of peace which should interdict every species of naturalization, for he knows it to be a fact, "that these aliens have been the great cause of our troubles, and disgrace, and until the country is rid of them it will foster serpents in its bosom."

1. referring to one of the key figures of the French Revolution, Maximilien de Robespierre 2. The Embargo and Nonimportation Law was repealed on April 14, 1814. The law had been established in 1807 and banned all international trade in and out of U.S. ports.

A Violent People

Forty years ago the Tammany Savage Society, composed of Irishmen, denounced President [James] Madison, for having recommended to Congress the repeal of the embargo laws. At that period there were not two hundred thousand immigrants in the country, yet they were organized into societies and into communities, and were, says the writer, "the great cause of our troubles and disgrace." The immigrants of 1814 were far superior to those of the present day. They came to seek an asylum in this land of constitutional liberty, and not to govern it; they came to enjoy the blessings of our laws and not to make laws; but even then so thoroughly had they imbibed the sympathies and feelings and principles of their respective races, that it was impossible to divest themselves of them. Since then the races have degenerated, and the immigrants of the present day are but the inferior specimens of these degenerated races. The Dublin "Evening Alail" of April 13th, 1855, contains an account of a recent election in Cavant County, Ireland, which furnishes us with a striking illustration of the character of the Irish elector at home. It says:

> A body of upwards of two thousand men marched into the town, brandishing formidable sticks, in a truly independent manner, and shouting for the tenant right and Hughes. Three Roman Catholic clergymen accompanied them, on horseback, and also, it was stated, ninety voters for Mr. Hughes. Other large bodies followed in quick succession, and the approach to the court-house was soon almost blocked up—the aspect of affairs which had previously worn a rather quiet appearance, becoming very visibly altered. A lane was formed of fellows brandishing their sticks, through which the voters going to the court-house were obliged to pass. The position of soldiers and the police, was somewhat altered, in order to keep this mob back. After a while they began to seize voters and drag them into Mr. Hughes's committee rooms.
>
> A party of armed men went, between nine and ten

o'clock on Tuesday night, to the house of an elector at Ballinagh, for the purpose of making him promise to vote for Mr. Hughes. He refused to do so, and then they demanded that he should swear not to vote for Mr. Burrowes, and on his refusing this also, THEY THREW HIM ACROSS THE FIRE, AND HELD HIM THERE UNTIL THE FLESH WAS BURNED OFF HIS RIBS.

The Catholic party endeavored to force a man named John Corr to vote against his conscience. After being imprisoned and maltreated for two hours, the account says: "They put him on his knees, and tried to compel him to swear that he would not vote for Mr. Burrowes, but he resolutely refused to do so. They then dragged him back into town to the court-house, in the roughest manner and kicking him and knocking out one of his teeth. They detained a tally-ticket for him in the liberal committee room; he refused to take it into his hand, and it was thrust into his breast. He was then brought into the booth, but he objected to vote, on the ground that he had been kept under constraint; after sitting some time in the court-house, he was enabled, with the aid of a gentleman named Gaffney, to return to his home."

Seeking Political Power

It must be borne in mind, that these outlaws are the electors of Ireland, and claimed as the respectable and intelligent portion of the population. If they prostitute the ballot-box at home, what may we expect from the less intelligent and more reckless, who flock to our shores by thousands?

In late years, immigration has greatly increased. Foreign organizations have become more numerous and formidable, and their attempts to obtain political power more frequent. At a charter election, held in the city of New York, a few years ago, the following hand-bill was published by the Irish organization, and extensively circulated, to wit:

Irishmen to your post, or you will lose America. By perseverance you may become its rulers. By negligence you will become its slaves. Your own country was lost by submitting to ambitious rulers. This beautiful country you gain by being firm and united. Vote the tickets Alexander Stewart, Alderman; Edward Flannigan, Assessor, both true Irishmen.

About the same time, at an election in the county of Lasalle, Illinois, a body of Irish immigrants, numbering about two thousand, brought forward and supported an Irishman for the office of sheriff, in opposition to all American of the same national politics, and of much longer residence in the country, and elected him, by upwards of one thousand majority.

In the town of Patterson, New Jersey, but a few years ago, an election was held, in which the foreigners elected thirty-three out of thirty-seven township officers. Numerous instances could be cited where the leaders of political parties have been compelled to submit to the decision of the foreign population of their respective election districts, which of the candidates should be run by their party for an office; and the political history of our country, for a few years back, is full of instances, in which the foreign organizations have demanded of the candidates pledges.

Chinese Immigrants Deserve Respect

MARK TWAIN

Chinese immigrants in the nineteenth century settled primarily in California and Nevada, many of them working on the railroads or in mining towns. In the following excerpt from his travelogue, Roughing It, *Mark Twain details his experiences in the Chinese quarter of Virginia City, Nevada. He decries the abuse of Chinese immigrants, asserting that they are an inoffensive and hard-working people. In his visits to various stores in the Chinese neighborhood, Twain describes the hospitability and industriousness of the shopkeepers. Twain concludes that Chinese immigrants are worthy of respect; only the lowest classes, police, and politicians treat the Chinese poorly, he asserts. Twain, born Samuel Clemens, is one of America's most revered writers. He wrote humorous stories, novels, and nonfiction works, including* Roughing It, *an account of his travels in the western United States.*

O f course there was a large Chinese population in Virginia City [Nevada]—it is the case with every town and city on the Pacific coast. They are a harmless race when white men either let them alone or treat them no worse than dogs; in fact, they are almost entirely harmless anyhow, for they seldom think of resenting the vilest insults or the cruelest injuries. They are quiet, peaceable, tractable, free from drunkenness, and they are as industrious as the day is long. A disorderly Chinaman is rare, and

Mark Twain, *Roughing It, Volume II*, 1871.

a lazy one does not exist. So long as a Chinaman has strength to use his hands he needs no support from anybody; white men often complain of want of work, but a Chinaman offers no such complaint; he always manages to find something to do. He is a great convenience to everybody—even to the worst class of white men, for he bears the most of their sins, suffering fines for their petty thefts, imprisonment for their robberies, and death for their murders. Any white man can swear a Chinaman's life away in the courts, but no Chinaman can testify against a white man. Ours is the "land of the free"—nobody denies that—nobody challenges it. [Maybe it is because we won't let other people testify.] As I write, news comes that in broad daylight in San Francisco, some boys have stoned an inoffensive Chinaman to death, and that although a large crowd witnessed the shameful deed, no one interfered.

Industrious and Intelligent

There are seventy thousand (and possibly one hundred thousand) Chinamen on the Pacific coast. There were about a thousand in Virginia. They were penned into a "Chinese quarter"—a thing which they do not particularly object to, as they are fond of herding together. Their buildings were of wood; usually only one story high, and set thickly together along streets scarcely wide enough for a wagon to pass through. Their quarter was a little removed from the rest of the town. The chief employment of Chinamen in towns is to wash clothing. They always send a bill pinned to the clothes. It is mere ceremony, for it does not enlighten the customer much. Their price for washing was $2.50 per dozen—rather cheaper than white people could afford to wash for at that time. A very common sign on the Chinese houses was: "See Yup, Washer and Ironer"; "Hong Wo, Washer"; "Sam Sing & Ah Hop, Washing." The house-servants, cooks, etc., in California and Nevada, were chiefly Chinamen. There were few white servants and no China-women so employed. Chinamen make good house-servants, being quick, obedient, patient, quick to learn, and tirelessly industrious. They do not need to be taught a thing twice, as a general thing. They are imitative. If a Chinaman were to see his master break up a center-table, in a passion, and kindle a fire with it, that Chinaman would be likely to resort to the furniture for fuel forever afterward.

All Chinamen can read, write, and cipher with easy facility—pity but all our petted voters could. In California they rent little patches of ground and do a deal of gardening. They will raise surprising crops of vegetables on a sand-pile. They waste nothing. What is rubbish to a Christian, a Chinaman carefully preserves and makes useful in one way or another. He gathers up all the old oyster and sardine cans that white people throw away, and procures marketable tin and solder from them by melting. He gathers up old bones and turns them into manure. In California he gets a living out of old mining claims that white men have abandoned as exhausted and worthless—and then the officers come down on him once a month with an exorbitant swindle to which the legislature has given the broad, general name of "foreign" mining tax, but it is usually inflicted on no foreigners but Chinamen. This swindle has in some cases been repeated once or twice on the same victim in the course of the same month—but the public treasury was not additionally enriched by it, probably.

Attitudes Toward Death

Chinamen hold their dead in great reverence—they worship their departed ancestors, in fact. Hence, in China, a man's front yard, back yard, or any other part of his premises, is made his family burying-ground, in order that he may visit the graves at any and all times. Therefore that huge empire is one mighty cemetery; it is ridged and wrinkled from its center to its circumference with graves—and inasmuch as every foot of ground must be made to do its utmost, in China, lest the swarming population suffer for food, the very graves are cultivated and yield a harvest, custom holding this to be no dishonor to the dead. Since the departed are held in such worshipful reverence, a Chinaman cannot bear that any indignity be offered the places where they sleep. Mr. Burlingame said that herein lay China's bitter opposition to railroads; a road could not be built anywhere in the empire without disturbing the graves of their ancestors or friends.

A Chinaman hardly believes he could enjoy the hereafter except his body lay in his beloved China; also, he desires to receive, himself, after death, that worship with which he has honored his dead that preceded him. Therefore, if he visits a foreign country, he makes arrangements to have his bones returned to China in case he dies; if he hires to go to a foreign country on a labor contract, there is always a stipulation that his body shall be taken back to China if he dies; if the government sells a gang of coolies to a foreigner for the usual five-year term, it is specified in the contract that their bodies shall be restored to China in case of death. On the Pacific coast the Chinamen all belong to one or another of several great companies or organizations, and these companies keep track of their members, register their names, and ship their bodies home when they die. The See Yup Company is held to be the largest of these. The Ning Yeong Company is next, and numbers eighteen thousand members on the coast. Its headquarters are at San Francisco, where it has a costly temple, several great officers (one of whom keeps regal state in seclusion and cannot be approached by common humanity), and a numerous priesthood. In it I was shown a register of its members, with the dead and the date of their shipment to China duly marked. Every ship that sails from San Francisco carries away a heavy freight of Chinese corpses—or did, at least, until the legislature, with an ingenious refinement of Christian cruelty, forbade the shipments, as a neat underhanded way of deterring Chinese immigration. The bill was offered, whether it passed or not. It is my impression that it passed. There was another bill—it became a law—compelling every incoming Chinaman to be vaccinated on the wharf and pay a duly-appointed quack (no decent doctor would defile himself with such legalized robbery) ten dollars for it. As few importers of Chinese would want to go to an expense like that, the lawmakers thought this would be another heavy blow to Chinese immigration.

A Trip Through a Chinese Neighborhood

What the Chinese quarter of Virginia [City] was like—or indeed, what the Chinese quarter of any Pacific coast town was and is like—may be gathered from this item which I printed in the [*Virginia City Territorial Enterprise*] while reporting for that paper:

> Chinatown.—Accompanied by a fellow-reporter, we made a trip through our Chinese quarter the other night. The Chinese have built their portion of the city to suit themselves; and as they keep neither carriages nor wagons, their streets are not wide enough, as a general thing, to admit of the passage of vehicles. At ten o'clock at night the Chinaman may be seen in all his glory. In every little cooped-up, dingy cavern of a hut, faint with the odor of burning Josh-lights and with nothing to see the gloom by save the sickly, guttering tallow candle, were two or three yellow, long-tailed vagabonds, coiled up on a sort of short truckle-bed, smoking opium, motionless and with their lusterless eyes turned inward from excess of satisfaction—or rather the recent smoker looks thus, immediately after having passed the pipe to his neighbor—for opium-smoking is a comfortless operation, and requires constant attention. A lamp sits on the bed, the length of the long pipe-stem from the smoker's mouth; he puts a pellet of opium on the end of a wire, sets it on fire, and plasters it into the pipe much as a Christian would fill a hole with putty; then he applies the bowl to the lamp and proceeds to smoke—and the stewing and frying of the drug and the gurgling of the juices in the stem would well-nigh turn the stomach of a statue. John likes it, though; it soothes him; he takes about two dozen whiffs, and then rolls over to dream, Heaven only

knows what, for we could not imagine by looking at the soggy creature. Possibly in his visions he travels far away from the gross world and his regular washing, and feasts on succulent rats and birds'-nests in Paradise.

Mr. Ah Sing keeps a general grocery and provision store at No. 13 Wang Street. He lavished his hospitality upon our party in the friendliest way. He had various kinds of colored and colorless wines and brandies, with unpronounceable names, imported from China in little crockery jugs, and which he offered to us in dainty little miniature wash-basins of porcelain. He offered us a mess of birds'-nests; also, small, neat sausages, of which we could have swallowed several yards if we had chosen to try, but we suspected that each link contained the corpse of a mouse, and therefore refrained. Mr. Sing had in his store a thousand articles of merchandise, curious to behold, impossible to imagine the uses of, and beyond our ability to describe.

His ducks, however, and his eggs, we could understand; the former were split open and flattened out like codfish, and came from China in that shape, and the latter were plastered over with some kind of paste which kept them fresh and palatable through the long voyage.

We found Mr. Hong Wo, No. 37 Chow-chow Street, making up a lottery scheme—in fact, we found a dozen others occupied in the same way in various parts of the quarter, for about every third Chinaman runs a lottery, and the balance of the tribe "buck" at it. "Tom," who speaks faultless English, and used to be chief and only cook to the *Territorial Enterprise*, when the establishment kept bachelor's hall two years ago, said that "Sometime Chinaman buy ticket one dollar hap, ketch um two tree hundred, sometime no ketch um anything; lottery like one man fight um seventy—maybe he whip, maybe he get whip herself, welly good." However, the percentage being sixty-nine against him, the chances are, as a general thing, that "he get whip herself." We could not see that these lotteries differed in any respect from our own, save that the figures being Chinese, no ignorant white man might ever hope to succeed in telling "t'other from which"; the manner of drawing is similar to ours.

Mr. See Yup keeps a fancy store on Live Fox Street. He sold us fans of white feathers, gorgeously ornamented; perfumery that smelled like Limburger cheese, Chinese pens, and watch-charms made of a stone unscratchable with steel instruments, yet polished and tinted like the inner coat of a sea-shell. As tokens of his esteem, See Yup presented the party with gaudy plumes made of gold tinsel and trimmed with peacocks' feathers.

We ate chow-chow with chop-sticks in the celestial restaurants; our comrade chided the moon-eyed damsels in front of the houses for their want of feminine reserve; we received protecting Josh-lights from our hosts and "dickered" for a pagan god or two. Finally, we were impressed with the genius of a Chinese bookkeeper; he figured up his accounts on a machine like a gridiron with buttons strung on its bars; the different rows represented units, tens, hundreds, and thousands. He fingered them with incredible rapidity—in fact, he pushed them from place to place as fast as a musical professor's fingers travel over the keys of a piano.

They are a kindly-disposed, well-meaning race, and are respected and well treated by the upper classes, all over the Pacific coast. No Californian gentleman or lady ever abuses or oppresses a Chinaman, under any circumstances, an explanation that seems to be much needed in the East. Only the scum of the population do it—they and their children; they, and, naturally and consistently, the policemen and politicians, likewise, for these are the dust-licking pimps and slaves of the scum, there as well as elsewhere in America.

Adjusting to Life in an Internment Camp

JEANNE WAKATSUKI HOUSTON AND JAMES D. HOUSTON

The United States has not always been welcoming to immigrants, a fact made clear during World War II. Fears that Japanese immigrants were not loyal to the United States and were working on behalf of the Japanese military prompted President Franklin D. Roosevelt to sign Executive Order 9066 on February 19, 1942. The order authorized the evacuation of all Japanese Americans living on the West Coast. These evacuees were sent to camps in the Southwest, where most of them lived until the war ended.

In the following selection, excerpted from a 1972 book written by Jeanne Wakatsuki Houston and her husband James D. Houston, Jeanne Houston describes how she and her family made the best of a difficult situation and gradually adjusted to life at the Manzanar relocation camp in Owens Valley, California. According to Houston, the camp residents learned to focus on enhancing the quality of their lives through art and gardening. She also details how the camps began to resemble average American small towns and how the teenagers enjoyed popular music and culture. Houston explains that by making their lives as normal as possible, the internees were able to forget about the war and their mistreatment by the American government. The Houstons are the co-authors of the memoir Farewell to Manzanar, *the source of this viewpoint.*

In Spanish, Manzanar means "apple orchard." Great stretches of Owens Valley were once green with orchards and alfalfa fields. It has been a desert ever since its water started flowing south into Los Angeles, sometime during the twenties. But a few rows of untended pear and apple trees were still growing there when the camp opened, where a shallow water table had kept them alive. In the spring of 1943 we moved to block 28, right up next to one of the old pear orchards. That's where we stayed until the end of the war, and those trees stand in my memory for the turning of our life in camp, from the outrageous to the tolerable.

Papa pruned and cared for the nearest trees. Late that summer we picked the fruit green and stored it in a root cellar he had dug under our new barracks. At night the wind through the leaves would sound like the surf had sounded in Ocean Park, and while drifting off to sleep I could almost imagine we were still living by the beach.

Mama had set up this move. Block 28 was also close to the camp hospital. For the most part, people lived there who had to have easy access to it. Mama's connection was her job as dietician. A whole half of one barracks had fallen empty when another family relocated. Mama hustled us in there almost before they'd snapped their suitcases shut.

Creating a Living Space

For all the pain it caused, the loyalty oath[1] finally did speed up the relocation program. One result was a gradual easing of the congestion in the barracks. A shrewd house-hunter like Mama could set things up fairly comfortably—by Manzanar standards—if she kept her eyes open. But you had to move fast. As soon as the word got around that so-and-so had been cleared to leave, there would be a kind of tribal restlessness, a nervous rise in the level of neigh-

1. Japanese Americans with dual citizenships were asked to promise to follow U.S. laws and be loyal to America, not Japan.

borhood gossip as wives jockeyed for position to see who would get the empty cubicles.

In Block 28 we doubled our living space—four rooms for the twelve of us. Ray and Woody [the author's brothers] walled them with sheetrock. We had ceilings this time, and linoleum floors of solid maroon. You had three colors to choose from—maroon, black, and forest green—and there was plenty of it around by this time. Some families would vie with one another for the most elegant floor designs, obtaining a roll of each color from the supply shed, cutting it into diamonds, squares, or triangles, shining it with heating oil, then leaving their doors open so that passers-by could admire the handiwork.

Papa brought his still with him when we moved. He set it up behind the door, where he continued to brew his own sake [rice wine] and brandy. He wasn't drinking as much now, though. He spent a lot of time outdoors. Like many of the older Issei [first generation Japanese American] men, he didn't take a regular job in camp. He puttered. He had been working hard for thirty years and, bad as it was for him in some ways, camp did allow him time to dabble with hobbies he would never have found time for otherwise.

Once the first year's turmoil cooled down, the authorities started letting us outside the wire for recreation. Papa used to hike along the creeks that channeled down from the base of the Sierras. He brought back chunks of driftwood, and he would pass long hours sitting on the steps carving myrtle limbs into benches, table legs, and lamps, filling our rooms with bits of gnarled, polished furniture.

He hauled stones in off the desert and built a small rock garden outside our doorway, with succulents and a patch of moss. Near it he laid flat steppingstones leading to the stairs.

He also painted watercolors. Until this time I had not known he could paint. He loved to sketch the mountains. If anything made that country habitable it was the mountains themselves, purple when the sun dropped and so

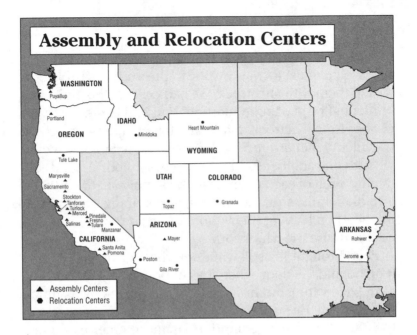

Assembly and Relocation Centers

▲ Assembly Centers
● Relocation Centers

sharply etched in the morning light the granite dazzled almost more than the bright snow lacing it. The nearest peaks rose ten thousand feet higher than the valley floor, with Whitney, the highest, just off to the south. They were important for all of us, but especially for the Issei. Whitney reminded Papa of Fujiyama, that is, it gave him the same kind of spiritual sustenance. The tremendous beauty of those peaks was inspirational, as so many natural forms are to the Japanese (the rocks outside our doorway could be those mountains in miniature). They also represented those forces in nature, those powerful and inevitable forces that cannot be resisted, reminding a man that sometimes he must simply endure that which cannot be changed.

Resigning Oneself

Subdued, resigned, Papa's life—all our lives—took on a pattern that would hold for the duration of the war. Public shows of resentment pretty much spent themselves over the loyalty oath crises. *Shikata ga nai* [It Cannot Be Helped] again became the motto, but under altered circumstances. What had to be endured was the climate, the confinement, the steady crumbling away of family life. But the camp itself had been made livable. The government provided for our physical needs. My parents and older brothers and sisters, like most of the internees, accepted their lot and did what they could to make the best of a bad situation. "We're here," Woody would say. "We're here, and there's no use moaning about it forever."

Gardens had sprung up everywhere, in the firebreaks, between the rows of barracks—rock gardens, vegetable gardens, cactus and flower gardens. People who lived in Owens Valley during the war still remember the flowers and lush greenery they could see from the highway as they drove past the main gate. The soil around Manzanar is alluvial and very rich. With water siphoned off from the Los Angeles–bound aqueduct, a large farm was under cultivation just outside the camp, providing the mess halls with lettuce, corn, tomatoes, eggplant, string beans, horseradish, and cucumbers. Near Block 28 some of the men who had been professional gardeners built a small park, with mossy nooks, ponds, waterfalls and curved wooden bridges. Sometimes in the evenings we could walk down the raked gravel paths. You could face away from the barracks, look past a tiny rapids toward the darkening mountains, and for a while not be a prisoner at all. You could hang suspended in some odd, almost lovely land you could not escape from yet almost didn't want to leave.

Small-Town Life

As the months at Manzanar turned to years, it became a world unto itself, with its own logic and familiar ways. In time, staying there seemed far simpler than moving once again to another, unknown place. It was as if the war were forgotten, our reason for being there forgotten. The present, the little bit of busywork you had right in front of you, became the most urgent thing. In such a narrowed world, in order to survive, you learn to contain your rage and your despair, and you try to re-create, as well as you can, your normality, some sense of things continuing. The fact that America had accused us, or excluded us, or imprisoned us, or whatever it might be called, did not change the kind of world we wanted. Most of us were born in this country; we had no other models. Those parks and gardens lent it an oriental character, but in most ways it was a totally equipped American small town, complete with schools, churches, Boy Scouts, beauty parlors, neighborhood gossip, fire and police departments, glee clubs, softball leagues, Abbott and Costello movies, tennis courts, and traveling shows. (I still remember an Indian who turned up one Saturday billing himself as a Sioux chief, wearing bear claws and head feathers. In the firebreak he sang songs and danced his tribal dances while hundreds of us watched.)

In our family, while Papa puttered, Mama made her daily rounds to the mess halls, helping young mothers with their feeding, planning diets for the various ailments people suffered from. She wore a bright yellow, longbilled sun hat she had made herself and always kept stiffly starched. Afternoons I would see her coming from blocks away, heading home, her tiny figure warped by heat waves and that bonnet a yellow flower wavering in the glare.

Life for Teenagers

In their disagreement over serving the country, Woody and Papa had struck a kind of compromise. Papa talked him out of volunteering; Woody waited for the army to induct him. Meanwhile he clerked in the co-op general store. Kiyo [the author's brother], nearly thirteen by this time, looked forward to the heavy winds. They moved the sand around and uncovered obsidian arrowheads he could sell to old men in camp for fifty cents apiece. Ray, a few years older, played in the six-man touch football league, sometimes against Caucasian teams who would come in from Lone Pine or Independence. My sister Lillian was in high school and singing with a hillbilly band called The Sierra Stars—jeans, cowboy hats, two guitars, and a tub bass. And my oldest brother, Bill, led a dance band called The Jive Bombers—brass and rhythm, with cardboard fold-out music stands lettered J.B. Dances were held every weekend in one of the recreation halls. Bill played trumpet and took vocals on Glenn Miller arrangements of such tunes as *In the Mood, String of Pearls*, and *Don't Fence Me In*. He didn't sing *Don't Fence Me In* out of protest, as if trying quietly to mock the authorities. It just happened to be a hit song one year, and they all wanted to be an up-to-date American swing band. They would blast it out into recreation barracks full of bobby-soxed, jitterbugging couples:

> *Oh, give me land, lots of land*
> *Under starry skies above,*
> *Don't fence me in.*
> *Let me ride through the wide*
> *Open country that I love. . .*

Pictures of the band, in their bow ties and jackets, appeared in the high school yearbook for 1943–1944, along with pictures of just about everything else in camp that year. It was called *Our World*. In its pages you see school kids with armloads of books, wearing cardigan sweaters and walking past rows of tarpapered shacks. You see chubby girl yell leaders, pompons flying as they leap with glee. You read about the school play, called *Growing Pains* ". . . the story of a typical American home, in this case that of the McIntyres. They see their boy and girl tossed into the normal awkward growing up stage, but can offer little assistance or direction in their turbulent course . . ." with Shoji Katayama as George McIntyre, Takudo Ando as Terry McIntyre, and Mrs. McIntyre played by Kazuko Nagai.

All the class pictures are in there, from the seventh grade through twelfth, with individual head shots of seniors, their names followed by the names of the high schools they would have graduated from on the outside:

Theodore Roosevelt, Thomas Jefferson, Herbert Hoover, Sacred Heart. You see pretty girls on bicycles, chicken yards full of fat pullets, patients back-tilted in dental chairs, lines of laundry, and finally, two large blowups, the first of a high tower with a searchlight, against a Sierra backdrop, the next a two-page endsheet showing a wide path that curves among rows of elm trees. White stones border the path. Two dogs are following an old woman in gardening clothes as she strolls along. She is in the middle distance, small beneath the trees, beneath the snowy peaks. It is winter. All the elms are bare. The scene is both stark and comforting. This path leads toward one edge of camp, but the wire is out of sight, or out of focus. The tiny woman seems very much at ease. She and her tiny dogs seem almost swallowed by the landscape, or floating in it.

Multiculturalism Harms America

LAWRENCE AUSTER

Liberals and conservatives have historically disagreed in their views on immigration; liberals largely welcome the influx of new cultures into the United States while conservatives prefer to preserve traditional American values. However, in recent decades the delineation between these two views has become less clear.

In the following selection, originally given as a speech before the Council for National Policy in February 2002, Lawrence Auster asserts that conservative support of what he considers left-wing immigration policy is helping to destroy traditional American culture. He claims that conservatives are too willing to accept the immigration of non-Europeans, even going so far as to extol the Hispanic culture that permeates American cities. According to Auster, immigration now has near-universal support in the United States because most Americans, regardless of their political views, believe that each immigrant can assimilate readily into mainstream American culture. However, Auster argues, many immigrants come from societies whose values conflict with those of America. He concludes that if the United States is to save itself from destructive multiculturalism, Americans must rethink their beliefs and write more restrictive immigration laws. Auster is an author whose books include The Path to National Suicide: An Essay on Immigration and Multiculturalism.

Lawrence Auster, "Mass Immigration: Its Effect on Our Culture," *The Social Contract*, vol. 12, Spring 2002. Copyright © 2002 by The Social Contract Press. Reproduced by permission.

The problem of immigration and the changes it is causing in our culture can be approached from many different angles. We could speak about the redefinition of America as a multicultural society instead of as a nation; or the permanent establishment of affirmative action programs for immigrants based on their race; or the town in Texas that declared Spanish its official language; or the thousands of Hispanics at an international soccer match in Los Angeles who booed and threw garbage at the *American* team; or the decline in educational and environmental standards in areas dominated by Hispanics; or the Hmong people from Laos who bring shamans and witch doctors into hospital rooms; or the customs of voodoo and animal sacrifice and forced marriage and female genital mutilation that have been imported into this country by recent immigrants; or the pushing aside of Christianity in our public life to give equal respect to non-Western religions; or the evisceration of American history in our schools because our white-majority American past is no longer seen as representative of our newly diverse population; or the vast numbers of Muslims established in cities throughout this country who sympathize with the Muslim terrorists and dream of turning America into an Islamic state; or *our own leaders* who, even *after* September 11,[1] keep telling us that the Muslims are all patriotic and tolerant, keep warning *us* against our supposed anti-Muslim bigotry, and continue letting thousands of people from terror supporting countries immigrate into America.

At bottom, each of these phenomena and many more like them are happening for one reason and one reason only—the 1965 Immigration Act which opened U.S. immigration on an equal basis to every country in the world, rather than, as in the past, favoring our historic source nations of Europe. Of course many of the recent immigrants from non-European countries have fitted into America and

1. On September 11, 2001, Islamic terrorists attacked the United States.

made good contributions here. It is the unprecedented scale of this diverse immigration that is the problem.

I could easily devote the rest of this article to making a detailed case that the post-1965 immigration is indeed changing our culture in negative ways. But here I want to ask a different question: Why have *we Americans* allowed this to occur? Why are we *continuing* to let it happen? And why, even when we gripe and complain about some aspects of it, do we feel *helpless* to do anything to stop it?

No Opposition

Many have argued, most recently [political commentator] Patrick Buchanan, that these things are happening because of the cultural left that hates America and wants to destroy it. There is no doubt that the cultural left hates America and wants to destroy it; and there is also no doubt that the left see mass immigration from Third-World countries as a handy way of achieving that. But that argument leaves unanswered a more disturbing question—why has there been no significant opposition to this leftist agenda? Presumably, the Republican party does not hate America and want to destroy it. Presumably, the conservative movement does not hate America and want to destroy it. Presumably conservative Protestants and parents' groups that have fought against Whole Language teaching and homosexual indoctrination in the schools do not hate America and want to destroy it. Yet nowhere among these legions of mainstream conservatives and the organizations that represent them have there been any serious calls to reduce this immigration from the non-Western world and the inevitable cultural transformations it is bringing.

Nor is the fear of political correctness an adequate explanation for this conservative surrender. Whatever the power of PC in our society, it cannot account for the fact that tens of millions of mainstream conservatives ranging from [radio talk show host] Rush Limbaugh fans to conservative evangelicals either support the current immigration policy or fail to speak up against it—even in the relative privacy and safety of their own organizations.

Embracing a Destructive Policy

We are thus left with a remarkable paradox—that the patriotic and Christian Right supports exactly the same immigration policy that is supported by the anti-American, atheistic left—an immigration policy, moreover, that spells the permanent eclipse of the Republican party and the victory of big government, since most of the recent immigrants vote Democratic.

Indeed, our conservative Christian President, when he's not busy embracing so-called "moderate" Muslim leaders who are allies of terrorists, wants to expand Third-World immigration even further. But that's not all. Unlike Republicans in the past such as Ronald Reagan, who supported Third-World immigration on the hopeful if naive assumption that the immigrants were all assimilating, President [George W.] Bush actively promotes the growth and development of foreign languages and unassimilated foreign cultures in this country. In a speech in Miami during the 2000 campaign, he celebrated the fact that American cities are becoming culturally and linguistically like Latin American cities:

> We are now one of the largest Spanish-speaking nations in the world. We're a major source of Latin music, journalism and culture. . . . Just go to Miami, or San Antonio, Los Angeles, Chicago or West New York, New Jersey . . . and close your eyes and listen. You could just as easily be in Santo Domingo or Santiago, or San Miguel de Allende. . . . For years our nation has debated this change—some have praised it and others have resented it. By nominating me, my party has made a choice to welcome the new America.

As president, Mr. Bush has not only left in place [Bill] Clinton's executive order requiring government services to be provided in foreign languages, he has started his own bilingual tradition, delivering a Spanish version of his weekly national radio address. Even the White House Web site is now bilingual, with a link accompanying each of the president's speeches that says *"En Español"* and points to a Spanish translation of the speech.

Yet, with the exception of one or two conservative columnists, these steps toward the establishment of Spanish as a quasi-official public language in this country have been met with complete silence on the right, even though opposition to bilingualism used to command automatic agreement among conservatives. If conservatives are no longer willing to utter a peep of protest in defense of something so fundamental to America as our national language, is there anything else about our historic culture they will defend, once it is has been abandoned by a Republican president?

A Quintessential American Belief

What all of this suggests is that mass immigration and the resulting multiculturalism are not—as many immigration restrictionists tend to believe—simply being imposed on us by the anti-American left. Rather, these destructive phenomena stem from *mainstream beliefs* that are shared by most Americans, particularly by conservatives. Of course economic and political forces, and the birthrate factor, are pushing this process in a variety of ways, but on the deepest level the cause is not material, it is philosophical and spiritual. The reason Americans cannot effectively oppose the transformation of our culture is that they subscribe to the belief system that has led to it.

What is that belief system? At its core, it is the quintessentially American notion that everyone is the same under the skin—that people should only be seen as individuals, with no reference to their historic culture, their ethnicity, their religion, their race. Now there is a great truth in the idea of a common human essence transcending our material differences. But if it is taken to be literally true in all circumstances and turned into an ideological dogma, it leads to the expectation that all people from every background and in whatever numbers can assimilate equally well into America.

This explains why patriotic conservatives acquiesce in a policy that is so obviously dividing and weakening our nation. Since the end of World War II, and especially since the 1960s, conservatives have tended to define America not in terms of its historic civilization and peoplehood, but almost exclusively in terms of the *individual*—the individual under God and the individual as an economic actor. For modern conservatives, what makes America is not any inherited cultural tradition from our past, but our belief in the timeless, universal, God-granted right of all persons in the world to be free and to improve their own lives. Therefore conservatives don't believe there can be any moral basis to make distinctions among prospective immigrants based on their culture.

We cannot say, for example, that a shaman-following Laotian tribesman, or a Pakistani who believes in forced marriage, is less suited for membership in our society than an Italian Catholic or a Scots-Irish Presbyterian. And we can't make such distinctions because, from the point of view of pure individualism, our inherited culture does not reflect any inherent or higher truth, and therefore cannot be the object of our love and protection. The only value that reflects higher truth and is deserving of our energetic defense is the freedom and sacredness of each individual. In practical terms this translates into the equal right of all individuals to make their own choices and pursue their own dreams, even if we are speaking of tens of millions of people from alien cultures whose exercise of *their* individual right to come to America will mean the destruction of *our* cultural goods.

An Act That Destroyed American Culture

In theory, multiculturalism is the opposite of liberal individualism. In practice it is the direct result of pursuing liberal individualism to its logical extreme. The 1965 Immigration Act was not about multiculturalism. No lawmaker said in 1965: Hey, we *need* Third-World cultures, we *need* female genital mutilation in our country, we *need* Shiite Islam and Wahabbi Islam to fulfil the meaning of America. The 1965 legislators voted to open our borders to the world, not because of a belief in the equal value of all cultures, but because of a belief in the equal rights of all individuals; the single comment most frequently heard in the Congressional debate was that prospective immigrants should be chosen solely on the basis of their "individual worth." But this noble-sounding sentiment was an illusion, because, in the real world, most of the people admitted into America under the new law did not come just as individuals. They came as part of the largest mass migration in history, consisting largely of family chain migration, and inevitably brought their cultures with them.

Thus, in passing the 1965 Immigration Act, we did two fateful things. We announced that we had no culture of our own except for the principle of non-discrimination toward people of *other* cultures—*and* we began admitting millions of people from those other cultures. We started letting in all these other cultures at the very moment that we had *defined our own culture out of existence.*

This delusional act led to the next stage of our self-undoing. In the late 1970s and 1980s, we began waking up to the fact that those other cultures were here, that they were very different from our own, and that they were demanding to be recognized and given rights as cultures. But at that point, what basis did we have to resist those demands? We had already said that the only thing that defines us as a people is non-discrimination toward other peoples; we thus had no justification for saying that maybe it's not such a great idea to import people adhering to radical Islam or Mexican nationalism into the United States. Having cast aside our own culture, we had no choice but to yield, step by step, to the elevation of other cultures. This is how America, through an indiscriminate and unqualified belief in individualism, ended up surrendering to its opposite—to multiculturalism.

Cultural Differences Cannot Be Ignored

What has been said up to this point will offend many conservatives, particularly Christians. For one thing, the Christian church consists of people of every culture and race, so why can't a nation? The answer is that the church is a heavenly organization, it is not responsible, as a nation is, for the defense and preservation of a particular earthly society. Mexico and Nigeria, for example, are largely Christian, but in cultural terms are radically different from the United States.

To believe that all peoples on earth should join our country is the very idea that God rejected at the tower of Babel. God said he did not want all men to be united in one society, because that would glorify human power. If I may presume to say so, God had a more modest idea of human life on earth. He wanted men to live in distinct societies, each speaking its own tongue, developing its own culture, and expressing God in its own way. This is the true diversity of cultures that constitutes mankind, not the false diversity that results from eliminating borders and coercively mixing everyone together, which destroys each country's distinctive character. Consider how today's multicultural London has lost much of its Englishness, and increasingly resembles multicultural New York.

So I would respectfully suggest that when Christians translate the spiritual idea of the unity of people under God into the political ideology that people from all cultures should be allowed to come en masse to America and other Western countries, that is not the traditional teaching of the Christian church, that is a modern liberal idea, that is the *Religion of Man*, which has been infused into the Christian church over the past fifty years.

But if this is the case, how can we reconcile our spiritual unity as human beings under God with our actual cultural differences? The answer is that in individual and private relationships, people of different backgrounds can relate to each other as individuals, without discrimination of culture and ethnicity. But on the group level, on the level of entire peoples and nations and mass migrations, cultural differences do matter very much and cannot be safely ignored.

It would therefore be a tragic error to limit our thinking about immigration to technical matters such as law enforcement against illegal aliens and security measures against terrorists, as vitally important as those things are. Beyond the immediate threat of mass physical destruction, we face a more subtle but no less serious threat to the very survival of our civilization. As Daniel Pipes writes in [a 2002] issue of *Commentary:*

> *To me, the current wave of militant Islamic violence against the United States, however dangerous, is ultimately less consequential than the non-violent effort to transform it through immigration, natural reproduction, and conversion.*

Of course I agree with Mr. Pipes. But, as I've tried to demonstrate, we cannot hope to stop or significantly slow that immigration unless we abandon this contemporary idea that America is defined by *nothing* except individual freedom and opportunity—the idea that America has no particular culture of its own that is worth preserving. Rethinking these beliefs and rewriting our immigration laws accordingly will not be easy, but if we fail to make the attempt, we will simply continue sliding, slowly but surely, toward the dissolution of our culture and our country.

Multiculturalism Benefits America

JOHNNY BURKE

The immigration debate of the late twentieth and early twenty-first centuries is nearly inseparable from the debate on the effects of multiculturalism, as immigrants bring with them languages and customs that are often starkly different from America's predominantly white and Protestant culture. In the following article, published in 1993, Johnny Burke considers the issue of multiculturalism and concludes that the cultural changes brought by immigrants are not a threat to America. Burke asserts that while cities such as Houston and Los Angeles have been transformed by the influx of Latino and Asian immigrants, these changes should not be viewed by European Americans as negative. He argues that Americans need to find ways for these many heritages to live together without any immigrant group losing its uniqueness. Burke concludes that "unity through diversity" will strengthen American culture. Burke is the chair of the political science and social science department at the University of St. Thomas in Houston.

M ulticulturalism will start a fight in an empty bar. Its extreme proponents offer little hope for constituting a common ground among different cultural groups; its extreme opponents fear that it treads upon the very ideals of Western civilization.

A lot more heat than light is shed in such polemics. And the fact is, there are undeniable cultural changes ensuing especially in such cities as Los Angeles, Miami, and Houston which have very little to do with assaults on Western civilization yet cannot be handled effectively by prevailing custom. Multiculturalism for an increasing number of Americans is not a cause, fad, or theory but a lived reality.

The Influx of Latin Americans

Houston, for instance, has been dramatically transformed by Latino and Asian immigration over the past fifteen years. In this citadel of Anglo-Saxon frontier individualism, no single ethnic or racial group now constitutes a majority. By century's end, in all likelihood, Latinos will be the largest group.

The sheer number of Latino immigrants continuing to stream into this country (the rate of which will not diminish significantly with NAFTA [North American Free Trade Agreement]); their geographic proximity to both Mexico and Central America; and the spread of Univision and other American-based, Spanish-speaking media means the assimilation patterns experienced by European-Americans a century ago will not be replicated. If anything, California, Florida, and Texas, among other places, will increasingly be imbued with Latino culture. As a Mexican-American on a *Frontline* documentary dealing with the L.A. riots commented: "We may not overcome, but we will overwhelm."

This does not necessarily threaten the American cultural consensus. Even if one has to speak Spanish at Wendy's to place an order, one still gets a Dave Thomas burger. Much closer to the bone, however, was the furor that arose in July [1993] over a citizenship ceremony in Tucson, Arizona, which was conducted in Spanish instead of English. These new citizens simply expressed their heartfelt fidelity to this country in the most meaningful way possible. Those who would question their patriotism should note that Mexican-Americans won more medals of honor in World War II than any other ethnic group.

Immigrants should learn English, for it will remain the language of business and political power in this country.

But why should they have to speak "English only" when English is not the language of choice on many streets? As Carlos Fuentes told Bill Moyers, "When you get a proposition in California to vote the English language as the official language of the state of California, this only means one thing: that English is no longer the official language of the state of California."

Adapting to Different Cultures

In the diocese of Galveston-Houston, parishes which are combinations of European-, African-, Asian-, and Latino-Americans are increasingly the norm, not the exception. Saint Jerome's Parish, where I have been facilitating multicultural relations, has Masses in Spanish, Vietnamese, and English. Although the English-speaking community (mostly European-American) founded the parish over three decades ago and remains its financial and leadership base, a quick glance at those presently being baptized, receiving First Communion, and being confirmed suggests that the parish is rapidly becoming comprised of first-generation Mexicans and Central Americans. The majority of the parish and 90 percent of the youth in religious education classes are Latino.

Given this trend, the question is not whether one will have to deal with multiple cultures, but how. Will it be in a begrudging fashion which at best tolerates the presence of "others" and otherwise begets hostility? Or will it be by creatively enabling these newer, growing communities to assume leadership roles without having to sacrifice their cultures?

Based on the latter course, [since 1991] I have coordinated the Saint Jerome's Multicultural Relations Committee, comprised of members from the parish's three language communities. We have no predetermined multicultural agenda, nor do other parish committees have to obtain our imprimatur before dealing with the multicultural dimensions of their activities. Rather, we simply discuss how to use our respective heritages to link rather than separate ourselves.

For instance, prior to the committee's inception, the pastoral council was largely comprised of European-Americans. The difficulty was that the nomination process reflected the manners of the English-speaking community: forms were filled out by individual parishioners two to three weeks before the discernment evening. The committee modified this format to include alternative channels of communication: with the Latinos, face-to-face communication at both the Sunday Masses and the charismatic prayer group meeting near the discernment evening; with the Vietnamese, given their hierarchical orientation, consultation with their leadership council. Subsequently, more Latinos and Vietnamese have both participated in the process and served on the pastoral council.

Essentially, the committee aims for an atmosphere of openness and trust that makes multicultural coordination of parish activities easier. When people are treated with dignity, given a chance to speak in their own way, and in return reciprocate with respect for "the other," cultural barriers can be broken down, if not overcome. And although the Vietnamese community at Saint Jerome's will be building its own church shortly—it has had a longstanding wish to form its own parish—better that such decisions be confronted in a forum of mutual understanding than left to the rumor mill of mutual misunderstanding.

All Cultures Can Contribute

The initiatives of one parish are hardly instructive for secular political communities whose constitutive groups are much more competitive and whose common "faith" is less clear-cut. But it is noteworthy that the city of Houston has turned to the Diocese of Galveston-Houston for assistance because of the diocese's concrete experience with multiple cultures.

Rather than necessarily being opposed to a moral consensus for America, advocates of a positive multiculturalism think that all cultures can in fact contribute to this consensus. For instance, in *The Good Society*, Robert Bellah argues that John Courtney Murray's *We Hold These Truths*—a text which reconciled Catholic natural law with the American compact—was the initial volley in a series of cultural challenges: first Catholics, then the civil rights, women's, and gay movements. The point is that inclusion in the political discourse need not be at the expense of abandoning one's cultural background. As pinpointed by a *Commonweal* editorial amid the sectarian atmosphere of the 1960 presidential campaign ("Catholics and the Presidency," January 1, 1960), are we to have "a pluralistic society with a strong Protestant tradition rather than a Protestant society with a pluralistic tradition?"

Unfortunately, most of the debate over multiculturalism gets caught in an either-or: either one maintains that there has to be a universal national identity to which one must assimilate in order to be an American; or one must maintain that our cultural identities are so diverse and autonomous that the best we can do is guarantee the integrity of each enclave and abandon any notion of a substantive common good. When culture is conceptualized as a "possession," one is left with either the uniform identity of the "melting pot" or the relativist identities of "separate-but-equal" cultural enclaves. But when culture is understood as a relation between people, a "gift" to be shared with others, then one can envision a moral-political community which neither assimilates nor separates cultural groups.

If multiculturalism were indeed just the most recent academic vogue, then it might be fun to engage in polemical banter. But the rapid cultural diversification in Houston and elsewhere is very real. The question is not whether we have to deal with multiple cultures but how: seeking "unity in diversity" offers a much more constructive approach at the grassroots level then either imposing a monoculture or rending our communities and nation apart in the manner of the Balkans. De Colores [the Colors of Christ]!

Immigrants Are a Vital Component of American Society

AMERICAN IMMIGRATION LAWYERS ASSOCIATION

The first major wave of immigration to the United States began in the middle of the nineteenth century. Since that time, critics of immigration have argued that these newcomers have been unwilling to assimilate. These analysts contend that immigrants refuse to learn English and that they create enclaves that limit their interaction with native-born Americans. As multiculturalism began to flourish in the 1990s, more Americans became interested in celebrating how a variety of cultures have shaped America. At the same time, many other Americans began to worry that such acceptance of other cultures was undermining traditional American ways of life.

In the following selection, published in 2003, the American Immigration Lawyers Association (AILA) refutes some of the most pervasive myths about immigrants, in particular the claim that immigrants do not assimilate. According to AILA, immigrants identify with American values and are eager to learn English. The association also points out that immigrants tend to be better educated than native-born Americans and that foreign-born Americans contribute greatly to the U.S. economy and to scientific research. Furthermore, AILA states that immigrants have served with honor in the American military. AILA is the national association of immigration lawyers and professors who teach immigration law.

American Immigration Lawyers Association, "Five Immigration Myths Explained," *AILA Backgrounder: Myths and Facts in the Immigration Debate*, August 14, 2003. Copyright © 2004 by the American Immigration Lawyers Association. Reproduced by permission.

Anti-immigration groups, in their efforts to further restrict immigration and oppose any positive reforms to our immigration system, often propagate myths to support their agenda. Several of these myths are addressed below—together with facts to set the record straight. . . .

Myth Number 1: America is being overrun by immigrants.

Myth Number 2: Immigrants aren't really interested in becoming part of American society.

Myth Number 3: Immigrants contribute little to American society. . . .

Myth Number 1: America Is Being Overrun by Immigrants

Here are the facts on immigration statistics:

> The number of immigrants living in the United States remains relatively small as a percentage of the total population. While the percentage of U.S. residents who are foreign-born is higher today than it was in 1970 (currently about 11 percent), it is still less than the 14.7 percent who were foreign-born in 1910.

> The annual rate of legal immigration is low by historical measures. Only 3 legal immigrants per 1,000 U.S. residents enter the United States each year, compared to 13 immigrants per 1,000 in 1913.

> The 2000 Census found that 22 percent of U.S. counties lost population between 1990 and 2000. Rather than "overrunning" America, immigrants tend to help revitalize demographically declining areas of the country, most notably urban centers.

Myth Number 2: Immigrants Aren't Really Interested in Becoming Part of American Society

Here's information about immigrants' feelings about the country and the future:

Immigrants are more optimistic about the nation's future. "A poll of Hispanics finds they are far more optimistic about life in the United States and their children's prospects than are non-Latinos," according to an August 2003 *New York Times*/CBS News poll.

Immigrants identify with America. "Nearly 70 percent of foreign-born Hispanics say they identify more with the United States than with their country of origin," according to the *New York Times*/CBS News poll. Only 16 percent, including those here fewer than 5 years, said they identify more closely with their native country.

Immigrants believe in the American Dream. A CNN/*USA Today* poll reported that more immigrants than natives believe that hard work and determination are the keys to success in America, and that fewer immigrants than natives believe that immigrants should be encouraged to "maintain their own culture more strongly."

Immigrants Are Learning English

Immigrant children learn English. In San Diego 90 percent of second-generation immigrant children speak English well or very well, according to a Johns Hopkins University study. In Miami the figure is 99 percent.

Naturalization rates are rising. Statistics from the 2000 census indicate a steady rise in the naturalization rates of immigrants. In 2000, slightly more than 37 percent of all foreign-born residents were naturalized, a 3 percent increase from 1997.

Immigrants want to become proficient in English. Reports from throughout the United States indicate that the demand for classes in English as a second language far outstrips supply. Data from fiscal year 2000 indicate that 65 percent of immigrants over the age of five who speak a language other than English at home speak English "very well" or "well." The children of immigrants, although bilingual, prefer English to their native tongue at astounding rates. In fact, the grandparents and parents of immigrant children have expressed some concern that their youngsters are assimilating too quickly.

Immigrants learn English. Only 3 percent of long-term immigrants report not speaking English well, according the National Academy of Sciences.

Myth Number 3: Immigrants Contribute Little to American Society

The facts show that immigrants contribute significantly to America:

Immigrants show positive characteristics. A Manhattan Institute report showed that immigrants are more likely than are the native born to have intact families and a college degree and be employed, and they are no more likely to commit crimes.

There are high levels of education for legal immigrants. According to the New Immigrant Survey, which measures only legal immigrants, "The median years of schooling for the legal immigrants, 13 years, is a full one year higher than that of the U.S. native-born." The New Immigrant Survey is a project headed by the Rand Corporation's Jim Smith.

Immigrants help with the retirement of baby boom generation. While countries in Europe and elsewhere will experience a shrinking pool of available workers, the United States, due to its openness to immigration, will continue healthy growth in its labor force and will reap the benefits of that growth. Federal Reserve Board Chairman Alan Greenspan has stated that "Immigration, if we choose to expand it, could prove an even more potent antidote for slowing growth in the working-age population."

Foreign-born expertise aids U.S. research and development. Foreign-born scientists and engineers make up 28 percent of all individuals with PhDs in the United States engaged in research and development in science and engineering, helping to spur innovation.

Immigrants contribute to entrepreneurship. *Inc. Maga-*

zine reported in 1995 that 12 percent of the Inc. 500—the fastest growing corporations in America—were companies started by immigrants.

Immigrants Help Defend the United States

Our understanding of the meaning of American patriotism would not be complete without considering the pride and commitment immigrants demonstrate on behalf of the United States. According to the U.S. Department of Defense:

> More than 60,000 immigrants serve on active duty in the U.S. Armed Forces.
>
> Immigrants make up nearly 5 percent of all enlisted personnel on active duty in the U.S. Armed Forces.

Nearly 7 percent of U.S. Navy enlisted personnel are immigrants. Historically immigrants have made significant contributions to the defense of America:

> More than 20 percent of the recipients of the Congressional Medal of Honor in U.S. wars have been immigrants, a total of 716 of the 3,406 Medal of Honor recipients have been immigrants.
>
> 500,000 immigrants fought in the Union Army during the Civil War.
>
> A special regimental combat team made up of the sons of Japanese immigrants was the most decorated of its size during World War II.
>
> Major U.S. weapons, such as a more advanced ironclad ship, the submarine, the helicopter and the atomic and hydrogen bombs were developed by immigrants.
>
> On July 3, 2002, President [George W.] Bush recognized the contributions of immigrants in the U.S. Armed Forces by signing an executive order that provided for "expedited naturalization" of noncitizen men and women serving on active-duty since September 11, 2001. The order granted some 15,000 members of the U.S. military who

served fewer than three years the right to apply for expedited citizenship in recognition of their service.

After the passage of Section 329 of the Immigration and Nationality Act, 143,000 noncitizen military participants in World Wars I and II, and 31,000 members of the U.S. military who fought during the Korean War, became naturalized American citizens, according to White House statistics.

At a time when Americans value patriotism more than ever, immigrants demonstrate that they are a part of this spirit through their service in the military. Paul Bucha, President of the Congressional Medal of Honor Society, has stated: "I put to you that there is a standard by which to judge whether America is correct to maintain a generous legal immigration policy: Have immigrants and their children and grandchildren been willing to fight and die for the United States of America? The answer right up to the present day remains a resounding 'yes.'"

Immigrants Are Part of America

In sum, who are these people we call immigrants? They could be your parents, your grandparents, your teachers, your friends, your doctors, your policemen, your grocer, your waiter, your cook, your babysitter, your gardener, your lawyer, your favorite actor, actress, or sports hero, your shopkeeper. Immigrants permeate the fabric of America. They are an integral part of our society, its goals and its values. The backbone that helps make this country great, they set us apart from every nation in this world. In short, they are us.

Many Illegal Immigrants Are a Threat to National Security

MICHELLE MALKIN

The terrorist attacks of September 11, 2001, were perpetrated by nineteen Middle Eastern men who entered the United States illegally. The attacks prompted a vociferous debate about whether or not America's immigration laws were too lax. In the following article, originally given as a speech on March 22, 2003, at a Cardinal Mindszenty Foundation conference, Michelle Malkin contends that the United States has failed to defend its borders against terrorists such as those who carried out the September 11 attacks. According to Malkin, illegal aliens with ties to terrorist organizations are being smuggled from Mexico and South America with the assistance of Iraqi natives. She claims that many of these illegal immigrants have attempted to bring into the United States biological weapons, an indication of the threat they pose. Malkin concludes that immigrants should be welcomed to the United States, but only those who respect America's laws and God. Malkin is a syndicated columnist and the author of In-vasion: How America Still Welcomes Terrorists, Criminals, and Other Foreign Menaces to Our Shores.

Michelle Malkin, "Invasion: How America Welcomes Terrorists," *Mindszenty Report,* vol. 45, June 2003. Copyright © 2003 by the Cardinal Mindszenty Foundation. Reproduced by permission.

My talk is about a serious subject and I open my remarks with a very different kind of prayer. It was a prayer that was recited by a stranger who was welcomed in America with wide-open arms. The stranger's name was Mohamed Atta. And the prayer was found in papers in his abandoned luggage after [the September 11, 2001, terrorist attacks] and it went like this: "Crave Death: Bring knives, your Will, IDs, your Passport, Oh God, open all doors for me; Oh God, you who open all doors, please open all doors for me. Open all venues for me, open all avenues for me."

Terrorists and Killers

At every twist and turn of his journey in America, the doors were opened for Mohamed Atta and 18 of his criminal associates. Unlike the millions of strangers who have come here to pursue faith, family, and freedom, the 9-11 terrorists did not come here to live the American dream; they came here to destroy it. These 19 homicidal hijackers came here seeking revenge, not peace. They came here craving death, not freedom. They were not the first to abuse our hospitality and they were not the last; they will not be the last to hide their evil intentions behind the disguise of benign visitors or needy immigrants.

My research highlights case after case of innocent lives lost at the hands of foreign terrorists and other enemies of peace who benefited from our broken latches, and our busted fences, our defective screen doors and the myriad other symptoms of lax immigration enforcement. Let us not forget the six people who died and the thousands who were wounded in 1993 at the World Trade Center during a bombing at the hands of illegal aliens from Palestine, Egypt, Jordan and Pakistan who freely overstayed their visas and exploited our loophole-ridden asylum system.

There were twelve people about whom I talk in my book *Invasion* who died from 1997 to 1999 at the hands of an illegal alien serial killer, Angel Resendiz, who goes back and forth freely across the U.S.-Mexican border. I don't have to remind you of the death toll on September 11, 2001, at the hands of Mohamed Atta and his terrorists hijackers who slipped past our snoozing State Department and Immigration and Naturalization Service [INS].[1] Five of those terrorists had freely overstayed student, tourist and business visas. Two were gunned down on July 4, 2002, in a very little reported act of terrorism at the Los Angeles International Airport. It was a lone Egyptian terrorist who escaped deportation when his wife won a visa lottery.

My home is in Montgomery County, Maryland, and in the fall of 2002 we were terrorized and ten people died at the hands of sniper suspects John Muhammad and Lee Malvo. Muhammad had been stopped in Miami for attempted illegal alien smuggling but was never prosecuted. Malvo was an illegal alien from Jamaica, who had been apprehended by Border Patrol agents in Washington State, but had been released pending deportation against the Border Patrol's recommendation.

An Influx of Illegals

A year after the September 11, 2001, terrorist attacks, we have new laws, we have new agencies, we have new government spending to fight off unwelcome invaders. But the Golden Door remains wide open to the world lawbreakers and evildoers.

Just a few facts. According to the INS, at least 78,000 illegal aliens from terrorist-supporting and terrorist-friendly countries live in the United States today. More than 300,000 illegal alien fugitives, including 6,000 from high-risk terror-sponsoring countries in the Middle East, remain on the loose in our country despite deportation orders. Last year [2002], at least 105 foreign nationals suspected of terrorist involvement received U.S. visas anyway because of lapses in the new background check system. There is still no systematic tracking of criminal alien felons across the coun-

1. Around three thousand people died in the attacks.

try, yet untold thousands of illegal aliens pass through the fingers of Federal Immigration Authorities every day. Even today, Mohamed Atta's deadly prayers for open borders and unobstructed avenues to terror are being answered by our government, which is supposed to be constitutionally bound to provide for the common defense. I believe that until our leaders, both political and religious, stop putting so many other interests above our national interests, a dangerous state of immigration and anarchy will persist.

Respecting God and Laws

As I prepared my talk, I came across some of Cardinal Mindszenty's living words that relate directly to the themes of much of my research and reporting. This is from His Eminence's 1974 book *Memoirs* and I quote: "In a country where the citizens fear God, they will respect the law. Where they respect the law, they will live in peace. A nation filled with peace is a strong nation."

My own journalistic interest in documenting the failures of border security and immigration enforcement matters is driven by both moral obligation and civic and professional duty. As a God fearing, law abiding, peace-seeking daughter of legal immigrants from the Philippines, I have never taken for granted the rights and responsibilities that come with citizenship. The oath, that my parents and so many millions of other naturalized Americans in this country took, resonated even more powerfully with me after September 11 than ever before. I'd like to quote from the oath that new Americans take. "I hereby declare on oath that I will support and defend the Constitution and the laws of the United States of America against all enemies foreign and domestic. That I take this obligation freely without any mental reservations or purpose of evasion. So help me God."

We cannot have a strong nation as long as we continue to tolerate massive undermining of respect for God. We all know that. But I also believe that we cannot have a strong nation as long as we continue to tolerate massive undermining of immigration laws. When scores of illegal alien day labors are allowed to congregate openly at fast-foods stores and near government offices, it sends a signal that no one cares. And that no one is in charge. It was exactly in this type of environment of chaos and immigration lawlessness that September 11 hijackers Hani Hanjour and Khalid Almihdhar were able to obtain fake photo ID's. From illegal alien day laborers hanging out at a 7-Eleven in Falls Church, Virginia, it was just a stone's throw away from the Pentagon where hijackers later crashed their plane. It was in this environment of bureaucratic sloppiness and neglect that all nineteen September 11 terrorists got away with filing incomplete visa applications in clear violation of our law and our sovereignty. It was in an uncontrolled environment that a total of 21 out of 48 Islamic radicals entered our country during the past decade. They broke our immigration laws with terrorist plots from the 1993 World Trade Center bombing to the New York City subway bombing conspiracy, to LA International Airport Millennium plot, to the September 11 attacks. They stowed away on ships, they overstayed their visas, and they committed marriage fraud, asylum fraud, document fraud and citizenship fraud to blend into the American mainstream. One of them, 1993 World Trade Center bomber Mahmud Abouhalima, brazenly filed a bogus application for amnesty under a federal program that was meant for Latin American farm workers. That is how Mahmud Abouhalima won permanent legal residence.

Smuggling Potential Terrorists

There are leading religious advocates of open borders, specifically our southern borders, who justify their defiance of Federal Immigration laws by invoking the biblical responsibility to welcome the stranger. They continue to argue that there is no connection between controlling illegal immigration and protecting national security. But the biblical precept to welcome the stranger must be informed by the stark post–September 11 realization that some strangers aren't here to seek shelter. Some strangers aren't here to do the jobs that no one else wants to do. These ill-willed strangers who have learned how to exploit every open door and every gaping loophole and every venue in our immigration system are here to do the job of slaughtering Americans of all faiths and backgrounds on American soil. Better intelligence and improved visa screening overseas will help screen out such unwelcome strangers, but we must shore up the home front as well. Putting out orange rubber cones to mark our borders as we do, even now along many parts of U.S.-Canadian land boundaries, is a farce. So is the ignoring of the dangers of massive unrestricted illegal immigration from Mexico.

How many [of Iraqi president] Saddam Hussein's sleeper terrorists are waiting in the U.S. right now to retaliate against us? How many [terrorist group] al-Qaeda arbiters line up moving comfortably and effortlessly in the interior of our nation and in states that give driver's license to illegal aliens and in cities that declared themselves as safe havens for illegal border crossers and for visa overstayers? I report in my book *Invasion* on an international crime ring that was led by an Iraqi native named George Tajirian; the crime ring demonstrates the scope of the alarming problem of potential terrorists pressing at our southern gate. The Tajirians guided aliens from all over the world into the U.S.—usually across the Rio Grande or through El Paso, Texas checkpoints, and arranged transportation and lodging for them once they were inside. According to federal prosecutors, Tajirian charged up to $15,000 a head. During his trial, which resulted in a thirteen-year prison sentence, prosecutors introduced evidence that he was responsible for smuggling individuals with known ties to subversive or terrorist organizations, as well as individuals who were known to have criminal histories. All told, law enforcement officials believed Tajirian and his Mexican collaborator Angel Melena, who was a high-ranking Mexican government official, may have smuggled more than a thousand Middle

Eastern aliens across the southwest front. The where-abouts of many of these smugglees remain unknown.

In early 2003, a Washington, D.C., jury convicted Mohamed Asane Housati for smuggling Iraqis into the U.S. through Columbia, Ecuador and other locations in South America. Housati supplied illegal alien Iraqis with stolen and altered European passports and round trip airline tickets to the U.S. in exchange for up to $8,000 per person. These Iraqi smugglees purchased documents at a commercial vendor in Northern Iraq called the Market of Passports which they used to travel through Turkey, Ecuador and then into Columbia. According to a statement from the U.S. attorney's office, Housati instructed the aliens to destroy the fraudulent passports and tickets while en route to America and to surrender to the U.S. Immigration authorities without disclosing their true place of origin. The whole scheme relied on knowledge of our government's catch-and-release policy. People are freed pending deportation proceedings and that policy remains in place today.

And yet, our borders remain wide open to infiltrators who may be toting more than suntan lotion and disposable cameras in their luggage. In March 2003, reports surfaced that up to half-dozen Iraqi illegal aliens had attempted to cross the Mexican border possibly carrying biological weapons. Opponents of stricter border controls insist that all we need to do to prevent foreign terrorists from striking again is to reform our intelligence agencies. They insist on only going after big obvious targets, suspected al-Qaeda operatives applying for visas overseas, and leaving everyone else who is breaking our immigration laws alone. But as long as the stubborn signals of an immigration system in total disrepair persist, the invasion that I described in my book *Invasion* will go on unabated. Such signals as driver's licenses for illegal aliens, in-state college discounts for illegal aliens, non-enforcement of employer sanctions, rampant asylum fraud, unpunished document fraud, sanctuary amnesty. Foreign terrorists will read these signals and accept our continued open invitation to enter through every available front, side and back door.

My thesis is that rampant immigration crimes are a result of unchecked border disorder, massive undermining of respect for the law. So-called small and harmless immigration crimes such as cutting through the rusted barbed wire, overstayed visas, committing marriage fraud, employing an illegal day laborer, lead to more serious national security problems. Examples are rampant of illegal alien gang activity, infiltration by terrorist's cells and internal corruption. First, one broken fence goes unrepaired, then vast miles of borders go undefended. First, hundreds of illegal border crossers go unpunished then millions of line jumpers win amnesty from Congress. First, thousands of visa overstayers are allowed to violate the rules without consequences, and then hundreds of thousands of fugitives from deportation are allowed to flout the law. Then the media stop referring to the illegal immigrants as illegal but use less judgmental descriptions such as undocumented worker, but that is inaccurate as many of these undocumented workers have plenty of documents. They just happen to be bogus and fake. Then cities begin declaring themselves as safe havens for illegal aliens (undocumented workers) awarding them free health care and voting rights, discounted college tuition rates and soon the INS commissioner himself is sending unmistakable signals to immigration law breakers that he believes that it is neither "practical, nor reasonable" to deport anybody for trashing our fences and our rules. Now untold numbers of radical Islamics have disappeared into the American mainstream. How did that happen? They are poised to attack both the figurative and literal foundation of our free society at a moment's notice.

Welcome Good Immigrants

In 1995, our Holy Father [Pope John Paul II] visited Newark, New Jersey, and he reminded us: "Quite close to the shores of New Jersey there rises a universally known landmark which stands as an enduring witness to the American tradition of welcoming the stranger and which tells us something important about what kind of nation America has aspired to be. It is the Statue of Liberty with its celebrated poem 'Give me your tired, your poor, your huddled masses yearning to be free, send these the homeless tempest-tost to me'." Is present-day America becoming less sensitive, less caring toward the poor, the weak, the stranger, and the needy? It must not. Today as before, the United States is called to be a hospitable society, a welcoming culture. If America were to turn in on itself, would this not be the beginning of the end of what constitutes the very essence of the American experience?

As a first generation American Catholic, I cherish the blessings of liberty each and every day. The American experience is alive and well in families, like mine, which count among dream-seekers from all over the world: Filipino, Italian, Scottish, Irish, Korean, Chinese, Hungarian, Russian, and that is just my immediate family! Yes, we should preserve a welcoming culture but not for Godless enemies of the American experience be they Communists, Fascists, or radical Islamics. Again to borrow the words of the Cardinal Mindszenty Foundation, those of us who share a common faith and love of country are bound by moral and civil duty to combine knowledge and action with prayer, penance and sacrifice, to defend Faith, Family and Freedom against those strangers who crave darkness and death over Pax and Lux [peace and light].

THE
HISTORY
OF
ISSUES

CHAPTER 2

Controversies over Immigration Policies

Chapter Preface

While most immigrants to the United States leave the countries of their birth voluntarily, others find themselves compelled to emigrate from their homelands in order to escape war, restrictive political systems, and persecution. The treatment of refugees at various points in American history provides insight into the policies that guide immigration policies. Regardless of the era, the welcome that refugees receive depends largely on how the U.S. government regards their nations of origin.

America's refugee policies prior to World War II were less than charitable, especially toward German Jews, who suffered great persecution under Nazi rule. Anti-Semitism was a serious problem in the United States during the 1930s, which helped to create a situation in which the *St. Louis*, a German boat carrying 933 passengers—predominantly Jewish refugees—was denied admittance to the United States in May 1939. The ship was forced to return to Europe, where most of its passengers eventually died at the hands of the Nazis.

The U.S. government became more tolerant of refugees in the waning months of World War II, establishing a War Refugee Board and a temporary haven for European refugees in 1944. Four years later the 1948 Displaced Persons Act permitted Europeans who had been displaced by the war to enter the United States. The act also allowed Chinese who lived in the United States and who could not return to China because of its civil war to receive permanent resident status.

Nearly thirty years later, the end of the Vietnam War brought a new wave of refugees. During the 1970s the number of Vietnamese living in the United States grew twenty-five-fold, from ten thousand to a quarter million. Like the Cuban refugees who fled when Fidel Castro came to power, these refugees were welcome because they were escaping a Communist nation. As anti-Semitism helped shape policy in the 1930s, so too did anti-Communist fervor influence immigration laws in the last half of the twentieth century.

American policies toward refugees have become stricter in the early twenty-first century because of national security concerns. Refugees and asylum seekers facing the greatest difficulties entering the United States are those from countries believed to represent a terrorist threat to the United States. Under the controversial USA Patriot Act, passed in the wake of the September 11, 2001, terrorist attacks, immigrants who are seeking political asylum and who emigrated from one of the thirty-three nations with known ties to terrorists are detained. The U.S. government has taken this precaution in order to be certain that these refugees are not terrorists. Under current policies noncitizens can be detained indefinitely if the government believes they are threats to national security.

At the end of 2003 the United States was home to 244,200 refugees and asylum seekers. Although not all of them will become permanent residents or American citizens, they exemplify the belief held by millions of immigrants that the United States is the desired destination when one is trying to escape persecution and violence. However, because the United States does not have open borders, immigration—whether for political, economic, or personal reasons—must necessarily be controlled. The contributors to the following chapter offer historical perspectives on the policies that have guided legal immigration.

Immigration Should Be Halted

FRANCIS A. WALKER

The U.S. government placed few restrictions on immigration during the first half of the nineteenth century. However, as the population of immigrants increased, especially from non-Western European nations, so too did calls for laws that would limit immigration. Several such laws passed in the latter decades of the century, such as the Chinese Exclusion Act of 1882, which restricted Chinese immigration, and the Alien Contract Labor Law of 1885, which prohibited U.S. companies from bringing in foreign labor.

In the following selection, an article published in the June 1896 issue of Atlantic Monthly, *Francis A. Walker, a high-level immigration official, asserts that immigration must be halted to protect the United States. According to Walker, the increase in the nation's population caused by immigration has reduced the amount of available farm land and created unemployment among native-born Americans. Walker further asserts that unlike the industrious immigrants of earlier decades, the present group consists of slovenly and violent failures. He concludes that unless the United States places a moratorium on immigration, the nation's social, political, and industrial institutions will suffer. When this article was written, Walker was the commissioner general of the U.S. immigration service and a contributor to* Atlantic Monthly.

Francis A. Walker, "Restriction of Immigration," *Atlantic Monthly*, June 1896.

The first thing to be said respecting any serious proposition importantly to restrict immigration into the United States is, that such a proposition necessarily and properly encounters a high degree of incredulity, arising from the traditions of our country. From the beginning, it has been the policy of the United States, both officially and according to the prevailing sentiment of our people, to tolerate, to welcome, and to encourage immigration, without qualification and without discrimination. For generations, it was the settled opinion of our people, which found no challenge anywhere, that immigration was a source of both strength and wealth. Not only was it thought unnecessary carefully to scrutinize foreign arrivals at our ports, but the figures of any exceptionally large immigration were greeted with noisy gratulation. In those days the American people did not doubt that they derived a great advantage from this source. It is, therefore, natural to ask, Is it possible that our fathers and our grandfathers were so far wrong in this matter? Is it not, the rather, probable that the present anxiety and apprehension on the subject are due to transient causes or to distinctly false opinions, prejudicing the public mind? The challenge which current proposals for the restriction of immigration thus encounter is a perfectly legitimate one, and creates a presumption which their advocates are bound to deal with. Is it, however, necessarily true that if our fathers and grandfathers were right in their view of immigration in their own time, those who advocate the restriction of immigration to-day must be in the wrong? Does it not some-times happen, in the course of national development, that great and permanent changes in condition require corresponding changes of opinion and of policy?

We shall best answer this question by referring to an instance in an altogether different department of public interest and activity. For nearly a hundred years after the peace of 1783[1] opened to settlement the lands beyond the Allegha-

1. ending the Revolutionary War

nies, the cutting away of the primeval forest was regarded by our people not only with toleration, but with the highest approval. No physical instrument could have been chosen which was so fairly entitled to be called the emblem of American civilization as the Axe of the Pioneer. As the forests of the Ohio Valley bowed themselves before the un-staying enterprise of the adventurous settlers of that region, all good citizens rejoiced. There are few chapters of human history which recount a grander story of human achieve-ment. Yet to-day all intelligent men admit that the cutting down of our forests, the destruction of the tree-covering of our soil, has already gone too far; and both individual States and the nation have united in efforts to undo some of the mischief which has been wrought to our agriculture and to our climate from carrying too far the work of denudation. In precisely the same way, it may be true that our fathers were right in their view of immigration; while yet the patri-otic American of to-day may properly shrink in terror from the contemplation of the vast hordes of ignorant and bru-talized peasantry thronging to our shores.

Two Opinions

Before inquiring as to general changes in our national con-dition which may justify a change of opinion and policy in this respect, let us deal briefly, as we must, with two opin-ions regarding the immigration of the past, which stand in the way of any fair consideration of the subject. These two opinions were, first, that immigration constituted a net re-inforcement of our population; secondly, that, in addition to this, or irrespective of this, immigration was necessary, in order to supply the laborers who should do certain kinds of work, imperatively demanded for the building up of our industrial and social structure, which natives of the soil were unwilling to undertake.

The former of these opinions was, so far as I am aware, held with absolute unanimity by our people; yet no popu-lar belief was ever more unfounded. Space would not serve for the full statistical demonstration of the proposition that immigration, during the period from 1830 to 1860, instead of constituting a reinforcement to the population, simply resulted in a replacement of native by foreign elements; but I believe it would be practicable to prove this to the satisfaction of every fair-minded man. Let it suffice to state a few matters which are beyond controversy.

The Demographics of Immigration

The population of 1790 was almost wholly a native and wholly an acclimated population, and for forty years afterwards immigration remained at so low a rate as to be practically of no account; yet the people of the United States increased in numbers more rapidly than has ever elsewhere been known, in regard to any considerable population, over any considerable area, through any considerable period of time. Between 1790 and 1830 the nation grew from less than four millions to nearly thirteen millions,—an increase, in fact, of two hundred and twenty-seven per cent, a rate unparalleled in history. That increase was wholly out of the loins of our own people. Each decade had seen a growth of between thirty-three and thirty-eight per cent, a doubling once in twenty-two or twenty-three years. During the thirty years which followed 1830, the conditions of life and reproduction in the United States were not less, but more favorable than in the preceding period. Important changes relating to the practice of medicine, the food and clothing of people, the general habits of living, took place, which were of a nature to increase the vitality and reproductive capability of the American people. Throughout this period, the standard of height, of weight, and of chest measurement was steadily rising, with the result that, of the men of all nationalities in the giant army formed to suppress the slaveholders' rebellion,[2] the native American bore off the palm in respect to physical stature. The de-

2. referring to the Civil War

cline of this rate of increase among Americans began at the very time when foreign immigration first assumed considerable proportions; it showed itself first and in the highest degree in those regions, in those States, and in the very counties into which the foreigners most largely entered. It proceeded for a long time in such a way as absolutely to offset the foreign arrivals, so that in 1850, in spite of the incoming of two and a half millions of foreigners during thirty years, our population differed by less than ten thousand from the population which would have existed, according to the previous rate of increase, without reinforcement from abroad. These three facts, which might be shown by tables and diagrams, constitute a statistical demonstration such as is rarely attained in regard to the operation of any social or economic force.

But it may be asked, Is the proposition that the arrival of foreigners brought a check to the native increase a reasonable one? Is the cause thus suggested one which has elsewhere appeared as competent to produce such an effect? I answer, Yes. All human history shows that the principle of population is intensely sensitive to social and economic changes. Let social and economic conditions remain as they were, and population will go on increasing from year to year, and from decade to decade, with a regularity little short of the marvelous. Let social and economic conditions change, and population instantly responds. The arrival in the United States, between 1830 and 1840, and thereafter increasingly, of large numbers of degraded peasantry created for the first time in this country distinct social classes, and produced an alteration of economic relations which could not fail powerfully to affect population. The appearance of vast numbers of men, foreign in birth and often in language, with a poorer standard of living, with habits repellent to our native people, of an industrial grade suited only to the lowest kind of manual labor, was exactly such a cause as by any student of population would be expected to affect profoundly the growth of the native population.

Americans shrank alike from the social contact and the economic competition thus created. They became increasingly unwilling to bring forth sons and daughters who should be obliged to compete in the market for labor and in the walks of life with those whom they did not recognize as of their own grade and condition. It has been said by some that during this time habits of luxury were entering, to reduce both the disposition and the ability to increase among our own population. In some small degree, in some restricted localities, this undoubtedly was the case; but prior to 1860 there was no such general growth of luxury in the United States as is competent to account for the effect seen. Indeed, I believe this was almost wholly due to the cause which has been indicated,—a cause recognized by every student of statistics and economics.

The second opinion regarding the immigration of the past, with which it seems well to deal before proceeding to the positive argument of the case, is that, whether desirable on other accounts or not, foreign immigration prior to 1860 was necessary in order to supply the country with a laboring class which should be able and willing to perform the lowest kind of work required in the upbuilding of our industrial and social structure, especially the making of railroads and canals. The opinion which has been cited constitutes, perhaps, the best example known to me of that putting the cart before the horse which is so commonly seen in sociological inquiry. When was it that native Americans first refused to do the lowest kinds of manual labor? I answer, When the foreigner came. Did the foreigner come because the native American refused longer to perform any kind of manual labor? No; the American refused because the foreigner came. Through all our early history, Americans, from Governor Winthrop, through Jonathan Edwards, to Ralph Waldo Emerson, had done every sort of work which was required for the comfort of their families and for the upbuilding of the state, and had not been ashamed. They called nothing common or unclean which needed to be done for their own good or for the good of all. But when the country was flooded with ignorant and unskilled foreigners, who could do nothing but the lowest kind of labor, Americans instinctively shrank from the contact and the competition thus offered to them. So long as manual labor, in whatever field, was to be done by all, each in his place, there was no revolt at it; but when working on railroads and canals became the sign of a want of education and of a low social condition, our own people gave it up, and left it to those who were able to do that, and nothing better.

We have of late had a very curious demonstration of the entire fallacy of the popular mode of reasoning on this subject, due to the arrival of a still lower laboring class. Within a few years *Harper's Weekly* had an article in which the editor, after admitting that the Italians who have recently come in such vast numbers to our shores do not constitute a desirable element of the population, either socially or politically, yet claimed that it was a highly providential arrangement, since the Irish, who formerly did all the work of the country in the way of ditching and trenching, were now standing aside. We have only to meet the argument thus in its second generation, so to speak, to see the complete fallacy of such reasoning. Does the Italian come because the Irishman refuses to work in ditches and trenches, in gangs; or has the Irishman taken this position because the Italian has come? The latter is undoubtedly the truth; and if the administrators of Baron Hirsch's estate send to us two millions of Russian Jews, we shall soon find the Italians standing on their dignity, and deeming themselves too good to work on streets and sewers and railroads. But meanwhile, what of the republic? What of the American standard of living? What of the American rate of wages?

All that sort of reasoning about the necessity of having a mean kind of man to do a mean kind of work is greatly to be suspected. It is not possible to have a man who is too good to do any kind of work which the welfare of his family and of the community requires to be done. So long as we were left to increase out of the loins of our people such a sentiment as that we are now commenting upon made no appearance in American life. It is much to be doubted whether any material growth which is to be secured only by the degradation of our citizenship is a national gain, even from the most materialistic point of view.

Land, Agriculture, and Labor Problems

Let us now inquire what are the changes in our general conditions which seem to demand a revision of the opinion and policy heretofore held regarding immigration. Three of these are subjective, affecting our capability of easily and safely taking care of a large and tumultuous access of foreigners; the fourth is objective, and concerns the character of the immigration now directed upon our shores. Time will serve for only a rapid characterization.

First, we have the important fact of the complete exhaustion of the free public lands of the United States. Fifty years ago, thirty years ago, vast tracts of arable land were open to every person arriving on our shores, under the Preemption Act, or later, the Homestead Act. A good farm of one hundred and sixty acres could be had at the minimum price of $1.25 an acre, or for merely the fees of registration. Under these circumstances it was a very simple matter to dispose of a large immigration. To-day there is not a good farm within the limits of the United States which is to be had under either of these sets. The wild and tumultuous scenes which attended the opening to settlement of the Territory of Oklahoma, a few years ago, and, a little later, of the so-called Cherokee Strip, testify eloquently to the vast change in our national conditions in this respect. This is not to say that more people cannot and will not, sooner or later, with more or less of care and pains and effort, be placed upon the land of the United States; but it does of itself alone show how vastly the difficulty of providing for immigration has increased. The immigrant must now buy his farm from a second hand, and he must pay the price which the value of the land for agricultural purposes determines. In the case of ninety-five out of a hundred immigrants, this necessity puts an immediate occupation of the soil out of the question.

A second change in our national condition, which importantly affects our capability of taking care of large numbers of ignorant and unskilled foreigners, is the [fall] of agricultural prices which has gone on steadily since 1873. It is not of the slightest consequence to inquire into the causes of this fall, whether we refer it to the competition of Argentina and of India or the appreciation of gold. We are interested only in the fact. There has been a great reduction in the cost of producing crops in some favored regions where steam-ploughs and steam-reaping, steam-threshing, and steam-sacking machines can be employed; but there has been no reduction in the cost of producing crops upon the ordinary American farm at all corresponding to the reduction in the price of the produce. It is a necessary consequence of this that the ability to employ a large number of uneducated and unskilled hands in agriculture [is] greatly diminished.

Still a third cause which may be indicated, perhaps more important than either of those thus far mentioned, is found in the fact that we have now a labor problem. We in the United States have been wont to pride ourselves greatly upon our so easily maintaining peace and keeping the social order unimpaired. We have, partly from a reasonable patriotic pride, partly also from something like Phariseeism,[3] been much given to pointing at our European cousins, and boasting superiority over them in this respect. Our self-gratulation has been largely due to overlooking social differences between us and them. That boasted superiority has been owing mainly, not to our institutions, but to our more favorable conditions. There is no country of Europe which has not for a long time had a labor problem; that is, which has not so largely exploited its own natural resources, and which has not a labor supply so nearly meet-

3. referring to an ancient sect of Judaism

ing the demands of the market at their fullest, that hard times and periods of industrial depression have brought a serious strain through extensive non-employment of labor. From this evil condition we have, until recently, happily been free. During the last few years, however, we have ourselves come under the shadow of this evil, in spite of our magnificent natural resources. We know what it is to have even intelligent and skilled labor unemployed through considerable periods of time. This change of conditions is likely to bring some abatement to our national pride. No longer is it a matter of course that every industrious and temperate man can find work in the United States. And it is to be remembered that, of all nations, we are the one which is least qualified to deal with a labor problem. We have not the machinery, we have not the army, we have not the police, we have not the traditions and instincts, for dealing with such a matter, as the great railroad and other strikes of the last few years have shown.

The Worsening Character of Immigrants

I have spoken of three changes in the national condition, all subjective, which greatly affect our capability of dealing with a large and tumultuous immigration. There is a fourth, which is objective. It concerns the character of the foreigners now resorting to our shores. Fifty, even thirty years ago, there was a rightful presumption regarding the average immigrant that he was among the most enterprising, thrifty, alert, adventurous, and courageous of the community from which he came. It required no small energy, prudence, forethought, and pains to conduct the inquiries relating to his migration, to accumulate the necessary means, and to find his way across the Atlantic. To-day the presumption is completely reversed. So thoroughly has the continent of Europe been crossed by railways, so effectively has the business of emigration there been exploited, so much have the rates of railroad fares and ocean passage been reduced, that it is now among the least thrifty and prosperous members of any European community that the emigration agent finds his best recruiting ground. The care and pains required have been reduced to a minimum; while the agent of the Red Star Line or the White Star Line is everywhere at hand, to suggest migration to those who are not getting on well at home. The intending emigrants are looked after from the moment they are locked into the cars in their native villages until they stretch themselves upon the floors of the buildings on Ellis Island, in New York. Illustrations of the ease and facility with which this Pipe Line Immigration is now carried on might be given in profusion. So broad and smooth is the channel, there is no reason why every foul and stagnant pool of population in Europe, which no breath of intellectual or industrial life has stirred for ages, should not be demoted upon our soil. Hard times here may momentarily check the flow; but it will not be permanently stopped so long as any difference of economic level exists between our population and that of the most degraded communities abroad.

But it is not alone that the presumption regarding the immigrant of to-day is so widely different from that which existed regarding the immigrant of thirty or fifty years ago. The immigrant of the former time came almost exclusively from western and northern Europe. We have now tapped great reservoirs of population then almost unknown to the passenger lists of our arriving vessels. Only a short time ago, the immigrants from southern Italy, Hungary, Austria, and Russia together made up hardly more than one per cent of [our] immigration. To-day the proportion has risen to something like forty per cent, and threatens soon to become fifty or sixty per cent, or even more. The entrance into our political, social, and industrial life of such vast masses of peasantry, degraded below our utmost conceptions, is a matter which no intelligent patriot can look upon without the gravest apprehension and alarm. These people have no history behind them which is of a nature to give encouragement. They have none of the inherited instincts and tendencies which made it comparatively easy to deal with the immigration of the olden time. They are beaten men from beaten races; representing the worst failures in the struggle for existence. Centuries are against them, as centuries were on the side of those who formerly came to us. They have none of the ideas and aptitudes which fit men to take up readily and easily the problem of self-care and self-government, such as belong to those who are descended from the tribes that met under the oak-trees of old Germany to make laws and choose chieftains.

Their habits of life, again, are of the most revolting kind. Read the description given by Mr. [Jacob] Riis of the police driving from the garbage dumps the miserable beings who try to barrow in those depths of unutterable filth and slime in order that they may eat and sleep there! Was it in cement like this that the foundations of our republic were laid? What effects must be produced upon our social standards, and upon the ambitions and aspirations of our people, by a contact so foul and loathsome? The influence upon the American rate of wages of a competition like this cannot fail to be injurious and even disastrous. Already it has been seriously felt in the tobacco manufacture, in the clothing trade, and in many forms of mining industry; and unless this access of vast numbers of unskilled workmen of the lowest type, in a market already fully supplied with labor, shall be chocked, it cannot fail to go on from bad to worse, in breaking down the standard which has been maintained with so much care and at so much cost. The competition of paupers is far more telling and more killing than the competition of pauper-made goods. Degraded labor in the slums of foreign cities may be prejudicial to intelligent, ambitious, self-respecting labor here; but it does not threaten half so much evil as does degraded labor in the garrets of our native cities.

Threatening Americans' Peace and Safety

Finally, the present situation is most menacing to our peace and political safety. In all the social and industrial disorders of this country since 1877, the foreign elements have proved themselves the ready tools of demagogues in defying the law, in destroying property, and in working violence. A learned clergyman who mingled with the socialistic mob which, [in 1894], threatened the State House and the governor of Massachusetts, told me that during the entire disturbance he heard no word spoken in any language which he knew,—either in English, in German, or in French. There may be those who can contemplate the addition to our population of vast numbers of persons having no inherited instincts of self-government and respect for law; knowing no restraint upon their own passions but the club of the policeman or the bayonet of the soldier; forming communities, by the tens of thousands, in which only foreign tongues are spoken, and into which can steal no influence from our free institutions and from popular discussion. But I confess to being far less optimistic. I have conversed with one of the highest officers of the limited States army and with one of the highest officers of the civil government regarding the state of affairs which existed during the summer of 1894; and the revelations they made of facts not generally known, going to show how the ship of state grazed along its whole side upon the rocks, were enough to appall the most sanguine American, the most hearty believer in free government. Have we the right to expose the republic to any increase of the danger from this source which now so manifestly threaten our peace and safety?

For it is never to be forgotten that self-defense is the first law of nature and of nations. If that man who careth not for his own household is worse than an infidel, the nation which permits its institutions to be endangered by any cause which can fairly be removed is guilty not less in Christian, than in natural law. Charity begins at home; and while the people of the United States have gladly offered an asylum to millions upon millions of the distressed and unfortunate of other lands and climes, they have no right to carry their hospitality one step beyond the line where

American institutions, the American rate of wages, the American standard of living, are brought into serious peril. All the good the United States could do by offering indiscriminate hospitality to a few millions more of European peasants, whose places at home will, within another generation, be filled by others as miserable as themselves, would not compensate for any permanent injury done to our republic. Our highest duty to charity and to humanity is to make this great experiment, here, of free laws and educated labor, the most triumphant success that can possibly be attained. In this way we shall do far more for Europe than by allowing its city slums and its vast stagnant reservoirs of degraded peasantry to be drained off upon our soil. Within the decade between 1880 and 1890 five and a quarter millions of foreigners entered our ports! No nation in human history ever undertook to deal with such masses of alien population. That man must be a sentimentalist and an optimist beyond all bounds of reason who believes that we can take such a load upon the national stomach without a failure of assimilation, and without great danger to the health and life of the nation. For one, I believe it is time that we should take a rest, and give our social, political, and industrial system some chance to recuperate. The problems which so sternly confront us to-day are serious enough without being complicated and aggravated by the addition of some millions of Hungarians, Bohemians, Poles, south Italians, and Russian Jews.

Arguments for Laws Restricting Immigration Are Prejudiced and Misinformed

ADOLPH J. SABATH

In December 1920 the U.S. House of Representatives debated H.R. 14661, "A Bill to Provide for the Protection of the Citizens of the United States by the Temporary Suspension of Immigration." The bill, which called for the suspension of immigration into the United States for fourteen months, with exemptions for close relatives of U.S. residents, was approved overwhelmingly, receiving 296 votes in favor and only forty-two votes in opposition. The bill was sent to the Senate, where it was modified, with the senators replacing the complete suspension of immigration with a quota system. The House agreed to the changes, and the Quota Act of 1921 was approved by Congress in May of that year. The act focused solely on immigration from Europe; the number of immigrants from each country was limited to 3 percent of the number of foreign-born people from that nation who were residing in the United States in 1910.

One of the few men who voted against H.R. 14661 was Illinois representative Adolph J. Sabath. In the following selec-

Adolph J. Sabath, address to the U.S. House of Representatives, Washington, DC, December 1920.

tion, excerpted from a congressional debate held on December 10, 1920, Sabath argues that support for the proposed bill is based on misleading information. According to Sabath, advocates for the bill exaggerate the number of immigrants entering the United States and wrongly claim that immigration will lead to rising levels of unemployment. Sabath further notes that immigrants are falsely labeled as charity cases. He concludes that rather than suspend immigration, the U.S. government should do more to help foreigners become American citizens.

From the hasty statements made by a number of gentlemen it would appear that there is no law against immigration and that all aliens can come in without restraint, regulation, or examination. Our present laws are strict enough in every respect. We now exclude idiots, imbeciles, feebleminded persons, epileptics, insane persons, paupers, persons likely to become public charges, professional beggars, persons afflicted with tuberculosis or a loathsome or contagious disease, persons mentally or physically defective, persons who have been convicted of a crime or misdemeanor involving moral turpitude, polygamists, anarchists, prostitutes, contract laborers, assisted aliens, and all who are admitted must have passports viséed by our consuls in the respective countries from which they come. . . .

Wild Misstatements

It is to be regretted that so many Members of this House should be misled by false statements relative to the tremendous number of immigrants coming to the United States. The only justification for such statements is due to wild, unreliable articles from men who willfully double and in some cases quadruple the number of immigrants that are coming. I regret that even the committee, due to the haste in preparing their report, should have fallen a prey to these erroneous, yes, false and misleading, articles. These statements and articles emanate from sources whose only aim is to mislead, prejudice, and alarm the American people. I have in my hands a report from the Secretary of Labor and of the Commissioner General of Immigration, which is marked "confidential," and which is not to be released until the 16th of [December 1920]. This report shows that for the fiscal year 1919 the total immigration to the United States was 237,000, while the number of aliens who departed was 216,000, an increase only of [21,000]. The same report for the fiscal year 1920, which ended June 30, 1920, shows that the total immigration amounted to 621,000 and that 428,000 departed, a total increase in the fiscal year 1920 of 193,000, and the majority of these are the wives and children of our own citizens and of those who have filed their declaration of intention of becoming American citizens.

These gentlemen are endeavoring to make the country believe that within the last few months millions of immigrants have come to our shores. I hope that the membership of this House will not rely upon the willful misstatements and articles of professional propagandists and paid lobbyists, but will investigate carefully all statements coming to them from such sources.

From the same sources come wild statements of the great unemployment which they variously estimate from two to four millions. These statements are just as unfair as those in regard to the millions of incoming immigrants. I maintain, though this is the slackest and dullest time in the year and that, due to the financial depression created by certain interests, there has been a lull in some of our industries and some lay offs of employees, but in a majority of cases it will be found that it has been done not because there is not enough work on hand but for the purpose of forcing down wages. It has been noticed in many instances within the past 10 days or two weeks that where lay offs have occurred the men have been re-engaged wherever possible at a lower scale of wages.

During the months of December, January, and February

we always find some people unemployed. This is due to the fact that many industries are at a standstill in the winter months, and to the further fact that thousands of farm employees, having no work on the farms, come to the large centers to seek employment during that period. But even with the influx from the farms and with the lay offs from some of the industries, I find in every newspaper of the large cities that there are three times as many advertisements for help as there are advertisements for situations wanted. Even if people are out of employment in certain sections of our country, I am satisfied that within three months there will be a greater shortage of labor than has been experienced during the summer of 1919 and 1920.

Stopping Immigration Does Not Benefit Labor

In the current number of the American Federationist Mr. Gompers, the veteran head of the American Federation of Labor, says:

> The world needs production. The employers have been saying so for months. They began with the armistice and continued until a few days ago. Now they have stopped saying so.
>
> The reason is not that the world's needs have been satisfied. The reason is twofold: Inflation is coming out of the business structure, and in the process employers see what they believe to be an opportunity to cut wages, though there has been no inflation in wages; secondly, the more unscrupulous employers believe that by laying off workmen with an announcement of curtailment necessities, the same or other workmen can be hired within a brief time at a sufficient wage reduction to make the temporary reduction justifiable from a profit point of view.

The following extract of a communication to me from the National Federation of Construction Industries speaks for itself:

It is evident that a proportional relationship exists between our national requirements for skilled labor and unskilled labor, over which we have no control except in so far as our inventive genius may devise tools of production by which the effort of labor is made more effective. Experience has shown that the law of supply and demand applies in employment the same as in the material market. If the supply of unskilled labor in the United States begins to exceed its proportional relationship to skilled labor, immigration automatically adjusts itself because of the decreased demand for unskilled labor. Any attempt artificially to regulate the fundamental law of supply and demand in the labor market through the restriction or stoppage of immigration can result only in national disaster; for it will be seen that, if immigration were to be stopped, the necessary proportion which must exist between skilled and unskilled labor, without which industry can not survive, could be maintained only by a curtailment of production to permit demotion of labor into unskilled capacities in sufficient numbers to restore the balance which must be maintained between skilled and unskilled labor. The direct result of such curtailment of industry would be disastrous to our national welfare for the reason that the law of supply and demand as it relates to commodities would operate to obtain a higher price level because of decreased production. . . .

In the interest of those who are so unduly alarmed as to the conditions and prosperity of our Nation, I have hastily prepared a statement which, if closely studied by these alarmists, will allay their fears as to the future and will compel them to wonder at the great strides our Nation has made in the last 50 years. It shows that though our population has increased threefold our wealth has increased sixfold, our exports twentyfold, and that the value of farm products has increased nearly tenfold. . . .

Misleading Statistics

For several days I have been striving to ascertain the source of the misinformation that has been used in arguments in behalf of this measure,[1] and not until to-day have I been able to find that they are based principally upon an article written a few days before the election by Frederick Boyd Stevenson. It purports to be an interview with Commissioner Wallis, who the writer states, has revolutionized Ellis Island [in New York Harbor, where immigrants are processed for entry]. It undoubtedly is from this article that the distinguished chairman of the Committee on Immigration and Naturalization and the other members of the committee who are advocating this bill secured their inspiration and information. I do not desire to make any charges or even insinuations as to why the interview was given or printed two days before the election, but I do charge that the gentlemen in using some of the guess figures of the contemplated or expected immigration and some paragraphs bearing on the class of immigrants were unfair not only to this House and the country but also to the commissioner. I make this statement because they have only used the most prejudicial statements and figures, ignoring completely whatever may have been stated in explanation.

The writer of the article states that of the 430,000 immigrants, 173,000 have no occupation, but he also states that 182,000 were women and children. Does he expect that all the women and children should have an occupation? He also lays great stress on the point that among these 430,000 immigrants an old woman 70 years of age came to a son, who had a wife and five children, and that should the son die, the five children, who no doubt were born in this country, and the wife and mother would become dependent upon charity. He does not know whether the son had property of his own, or whether the children may be of an age to earn their own living. In response to that statement I can not help calling attention to the fact that neither the com-

1. A Bill to Provide for the Protection of Citizens of the United States by the Temporary Suspension of Immigration

missioner nor the writer can point out many cases of those who become charges or dependent upon charity, and he will not find a single one of the Jewish race in a public charitable institution.

The gentlemen who have favored the passage of the bill and who have quoted from this article so frequently have failed to quote the commissioner when he stated that he is not a believer in the illiteracy test, and that a man may not know one letter from another but still make an honest and useful citizen. I wonder why they have not read that paragraph?

Encouraging Well-Intentioned Immigrants

It is gratifying . . . however, to find once in a great while a member of the judiciary of our country taking an interest in the immigration affairs of the Nation, and in this connection I wish to insert an editorial appearing in the *Chicago Daily News* of December 4 [1920] dealing with an address of Judge Evan A. Evans, of the United States Circuit Court of Appeals, delivered at Indianapolis, which shows that that able jurist has studied the question from an honest, unbiased standpoint, and that he has been able to discern the far-reaching effect upon our country should immigration be stopped. His suggestions of improvements in dealing with the immigrants and the means we should employ to assist them to more quickly become good and useful citizens of our great Nation in a great measure meet my views and should receive the attention and study of the membership of this House. I regret that time will not permit me to read the editorial, but with the permission of the House, I shall insert it in the RECORD:

JUDGE EVANS ON IMMIGRATION.

In the comparatively short and informal address which Judge Evan A. Evans, of the United States Circuit Court of Appeals, delivered at Indianapolis and which was published in the *Daily News* of yesterday were contained many valuable and thoroughly practical suggestions to Members of Congress and students generally of the twin questions discussed, namely, immigration and naturalization. In fact, a whole legislative program is outlined in Judge Evans's observations, which comprise six definite proposals:

Judge Evans believes in keeping the doors open to deserving foreigners, but he advocates the following notable improvements in our methods of dealing with immigrants:

More careful investigation of the qualifications of applicants for admission; provision for a five-year probation period for all admitted immigrants, they during this period to be required to learn the English language, under penalty of deportation for failure to do so; legislation expressly stipulating that naturalization is a privilege contingent upon good behavior, and that the commission of any one of certain designated offenses be made legal ground for the revocation of the privilege; a substantial increase in the naturalization fee, but not for the benefit of the Treasury.

There should be a national fund, Judge Evans asserts, for the sole purpose of assisting the newcomer to America from the day of his admission until he is settled and able to support himself in comfort. He should be protected from oppression and at the same time prevented from aggravating such evils as unemployment and urban congestion through ignorance or inertia. He should be directed to places that need workers and have undeveloped resources.

America is for Americans, Judge Evans well says, in the broad enlightened sense that only those who wish to become citizens and useful, honest members of the great community should be welcomed and permitted to stay. Those who do not value American institutions and are not appreciative of American advantages have no possible claim on the hospitality of the Nation. But there is still ample room for thrifty, upright, industrious, well-intentioned foreigners who desire to contribute to the welfare of the country while taking legitimate advantage of its exceptional opportunities. . . .

Were it not for the fact that I do not desire to abuse the privilege granted me I could insert hundreds upon hundreds of other letters, resolutions, and articles that have come to me within the last few days, protesting against the enactment of this pending legislation, but I have not heretofore and shall not now abuse the privilege. I also realize that it matters not what additional arguments, facts, and proofs I might submit it will have no possible effect upon the prejudiced membership of this House. As stated before, I feel that the Senate will not be carried away by this hysteria and pass the bill in its present form, but if that body should fall a prey to the propaganda now being carried on for this bill, I feel that President [Woodrow] Wilson, who history will accredit as the greatest Executive, statesman, and humanitarian, will, without doubt, refuse to approve such legislation.

America Should Have Opened Its Doors to Jewish Refugees

ROGER DANIELS

Throughout history politicians, government officials, and the general population have disagreed about which nations' refugees should be admitted into the United States. Such disagreement had disastrous consequences during the period immediately before World War II. As Adolf Hitler put into action his plan to expunge Jews from Germany, these unfortunate people began to flee their country. Unfortunately, many nations, including the United States, were reluctant to accept these refugees.

In the following excerpt from his book, Guarding the Golden Door: American Immigration Policy and Immigrants Since 1882, *Roger Daniels examines America's attitudes toward Jewish refugees during this period. He observes that although President Franklin D. Roosevelt was aware of the persecution of Jews in Nazi Germany, he made little effort to change immigration policies that made it difficult for Jewish refugees to gain asylum in the United States. Furthermore, according to Daniels, most Americans opposed helping the refugees. Daniels concludes that although thousands of Jewish refugees were able to reach the United States, thousands more could have been saved had Roosevelt taken action to respond to their plight. Daniels is an author and immigration expert.*

The "problem" of refugees from Nazi Europe, refugees who were mostly Jewish, arose only as the Roosevelt administration began. Viewed through the horror of the Holocaust, the callous indifference of the United States and the other nations of possible asylum has become a scandal with an extensive literature. But it is not really useful to view the policies of the 1930s, as too many do, through the prism of the Holocaust. Some of the literature can induce one to believe that Franklin Roosevelt and even Rabbi Stephen S. Wise were somehow responsible for the Holocaust. Authors of phrases such as "while six million died" create the false notion that the United States, merely by changing its immigration policies, could have saved all or most of the Jews of Europe, a palpable impossibility. Nor is it accurate to assume that the Holocaust was inherent from the moment the Nazis came to power. By the time Americans learned about what Walter Laqueur has called the "terrible secret" of the Holocaust, the fate of most of the Jews of Europe was sealed. To be sure, even at that late date more could have been done. If one wishes to make a judgment, it is hard to improve on Vice President Walter F. Mondale's, made in 1979: the United States and the other nations of asylum "failed the test of civilization."

Nineteenth-Century Attitudes Toward Refugees

Any attempt to understand the pitiful refugee policy of the United States in the Nazi era must confront American traditions about asylum and contemporary political and social pressures. Many share President Jimmy Carter's belief that the United States was and always has been "a nation of refugees," but such a conclusion is unwarranted. It is true, however, that refugees have been received, and sometimes welcomed, from the earliest years of the American experience. The assumption here is that a refugee is, in the common dictionary definition, "a person who flees from one's home or country to seek refuge elsewhere, as in time of war, or political or religious persecution." Protestant religious dissenters, Jews from Brazil, regicides fleeing the Stuart restoration, royalists and republicans, ousted slave-holders and Bonapartists, all found asylum here in the early years of our history. But these refugees were relatively few in number and greatly outnumbered by the 40,000 crown sympathizers, the so-called American Loyalists, who went or were driven into exile during and after the American Revolution. In the waning days of Federalism during the administration of John Adams (1797–1801), there was considerable concern about the subversive activities of some French, Irish, and British resident aliens. This, plus partisan political considerations, resulted in the passage of the short-lived Alien and Sedition Acts, which jailed some aliens for political activity and authorized deportations, but, in the event, deported no one. They surely made potential refugees wary about coming to America.

During most of the nineteenth century, few Americans voiced fears about political refugees, but despite the wide-open American door it was Britain that became the mecca for most European political exiles. The most significant exile activity in the United States was by Latin Americans, particularly Cubans who made a revolution against their Spanish overlords from bases in Tampa and New York.

Little Acknowledgment of Refugees

As noted before, in the early years of the twentieth century, political tests were being applied to immigrants for the first time. But, in the same era, the statutes that were designed to keep criminals out were carefully drafted so that "political offenses" could not be used as grounds for exclusion. In American immigration law there was no distinction between refugees and other immigrants, and the word *refugee* does not appear on the statute books until 1934, although in 1923 a "Near East Refugee Act" did pass the Senate. There was a clause in the literacy provisions of the 1917 immigration act waiving the literacy requirement—but nothing else—for "aliens who shall prove . . . that they are seeking admission to the United States to avoid religious persecution" but it is not clear that even one person gained admission because of that provision.

Roosevelt's Passivity

From the earliest days of his presidency Franklin Roosevelt was aware of the Nazi persecution of Jews, trade unionists, socialists, and others in Germany, and as a humane liberal Democrat he deplored it and spoke out against it. But for years he did little or nothing to change American immigration policy, either to restrict it further or to liberalize it, as many of his closest supporters wished him to do. When, for example, Felix Frankfurter and Raymond Moley urged him to send representatives to a 1936 League of Nations conference on refugees and appoint Rabbi Stephen S. Wise to the delegation, FDR instead took the advice of the State Department and sent only a minor functionary. In an election year he was willing to accept the narrow view of executive power set forth by Secretary of State Cordell Hull (1871–1955). This conservative Tennessee Democrat, whose wife was Jewish, told the president that the law left him "no latitude" even to discuss "questions concerning the legal status of aliens."

Similarly, when his handpicked successor as governor of New York, Herbert H. Lehman (1878–1963), wrote him on two occasions, in 1935 and 1936, about the difficulties German Jews were having in getting visas from some American consulates in Germany, the president sent replies drafted in the State Department. The letters assured Lehman of FDR's "sympathetic interest" and claimed that consular officials abroad were carrying out their duties "in a considerate and humane manner." In addition, the governor was assured that a visa would be issued when the preponderance of evidence supports a conclusion that the person promising the applicant's support will be likely to take steps to prevent the applicant from becoming a public charge.

Roosevelt was notoriously distrustful of the State Department, and letting its bureaucrats draft his responses shows that he simply did not want to interfere or even to know what was really going on. Our most activist president could be quite passive when it suited him to be.

There is irrefutable evidence that many State Department officials consistently made it difficult for most refugees in general and Jewish refugees in particular to gain asylum in the United States. One example involving just two individuals reflects a pervasive problem. Hebrew Union College (HUC) had a refugee scholars project, which between 1935 and 1942 brought eleven refugee scholars and some of their families to its Cincinnati campus. Although there was no question of any of these persons becoming a public charge, most were able to enter under a provision of the 1924 act which exempted from quota restriction

> an immigrant who continuously for at least two years immediately preceding [his visa application] has been, and who seeks to enter the United States solely for the purpose of, carrying on the vocation of minister of any religious denomination, or professor of a college, academy, seminary or university, and his wife, and his unmarried children under 18 years age . . .

This provision must have seemed heaven-sent to the scholars that HUC, the premier American institution for training Reform rabbis, was trying to bring out. But, as Michael A. Meyer, the historian of the project, has demonstrated, the State Department, in the person of Avra M. Warren, head of the Visa Division, consistently created difficulties, difficulties that in some cases proved insurmountable. . . .

A Paltry Response

Late in the 1930s the Roosevelt administration began to move on the refugee question, but its actions can best be characterized by the phrase that describes so much of Western democracy's opposition to fascism—too little and too late. Shortly after the *Anschluss*, the German annexation of Austria in March 1938, FDR created an Advisory Committee on Political Refugees under the chairmanship of James G. McDonald, former High Commissioner for Refugees of the League of Nations, and assigned an interdepartmental committee of government officials to work with it. FDR also instructed Secretary Hull to try to arrange an international conference to "facilitate the emigration from Austria and presumably from Germany of political refugees," adding the caveat, "No country would be expected or asked to receive a greater number of immigrants than is permitted by its existing regulations." He appointed Myron C. Taylor (1874–1959), former chairman of the United States Steel Corporation, to the rank of ambassador and named him to head the American delegation to the conference, which met in Evian, France, in July 1938. Its only accomplishment was to create an Intergovernmental Committee on Refugees, headquartered in London, under the chairmanship of George Rublee (1868–1957), an American lawyer. Just before the outbreak of war in September 1939, Rublee did manage to negotiate a sub-rosa agreement looking toward the orderly emigration of 400,000 Jews over a five-year period; the hostilities made it nugatory.

In his note to the appropriate volume of his papers, FDR wrote things he never said to the American people in the crucial years of the refugee crisis, 1938–39.

> For centuries this country has always been the traditional haven of refuge for countless victims of religious and political persecution in other lands. These immigrants have made outstanding contributions to American music, art, literature, business, finance, philanthropy, and many other phases of our cultural, political,

industrial and commercial life. It was quite fitting, therefore, that the United States should follow its traditional role and take the lead in calling the Evian meeting . . .

As this is written in June, 1941, it seems so tragically ironical to realize how many citizens of these various countries [which had been overly cautious in their attitude about receiving refugees] either are themselves now refugees, or pray for a chance to leave their native lands and seek some refuge from the cruel hand of the Nazi invader. Even the kings and queens and princes of some of them are now in the same position as these political and religious minorities were in 1938—knocking on the doors of other lands for admittance.

When one compares this account with what the United States actually did and did not do in the months before war broke out in Europe, it is difficult not to believe that a guilty conscience lay behind his remarks, which later would be easy to describe as hypocritical. Of course, Congress and the American people were opposed to any dropping of our immigration barriers, as both Roosevelt and his ambassador, Myron Taylor, knew. . . .

American Officials Ignored the Plight of Refugees

The American record, as opposed to its rhetoric and post-facto rationalizations, was dismal. Although we do not know how many actual visa applications by would-be German refugees there were—one scholar says more than 300,000 by June 1939—the fact is that between Hitler's coming to power and *Kristallnacht*, emigration from Germany was relatively light; . . . more than half of the German quota spaces for the period 1933–40 went unused. Thus a large portion of the Jews of Germany could have been accepted even within the relatively strict limits of the quota law.

The few attempts by sympathetic congresspersons to admit more refugees were forlorn hopes. The most notable of these was the so-called Wagner-Rogers bill of early 1939, which proposed bringing 20,000 German children to the United States outside of the quota system. Although sponsored by the New Deal's most prolific legislator, Senator Robert F. Wagner (D-NY), and a liberal Republican, Representative Edith Nourse Rogers of Massachusetts, the bill never came to the floor for a vote. It had a great deal of support from prominent Americans—including Herbert Hoover—but was opposed by a sizable majority of ordinary Americans, according to the public opinion polls. We do not know what would have happened had the White House tried to lead public opinion and put pressure on reluctant Democrats. FDR refused to do so. He was willing to allow some administration officials—Secretary of Labor Frances Perkins and Children's Bureau Chief Katherine Lenroot—to testify in its favor. Other officials, such as Secretary of State Hull, took no stand but informed Congress of the numerous administrative difficulties the proposed law would create. Roosevelt even told his wife, in February 1939, that "it is all right for you to support the child refugee bill, but it is best for me to say nothing [now]." Now became never. In June, as the bill was dying, the president annotated a memo asking for his support "File No Action, FDR." In addition, some of his personal and official family viciously opposed the bill: one of his favorite cousins, Laura Delano, wife of Commissioner of Immigration and Naturalization James Houghteling, told people at cocktail parties that the "20,000 charming children would all too soon grow up into 20,000 ugly adults."

One final pre-war episode, that of the German vessel *St. Louis* in May 1939, demonstrates the degree to which American officials' hearts had hardened against admitting any refugees outside of the quota system. The *St. Louis* was a Hamburg-Amerika line vessel bringing 933 passengers, most of them Jewish refugees, to Havana. Many of the refugees were on the American quota list but held numbers that had not yet come up. They and others came to Western Hemisphere ports to wait their turn. There were already some 2,500 refugees in Havana. Seven hundred and forty-three of the passengers had applied for visas and had the necessary affidavits of support. For reasons that are not entirely clear, the Cuban government refused to let the refugees land. Hoping to land those with visa applications in the United States, the vessel proceeded to Miami, but it was refused permission to dock. For a time it was so close to Miami Beach that the passengers could hear dance music being played at the resort's luxury hotels. That was as close as the refugees came to the golden door. The Treasury Department even assigned a Coast Guard cutter to shadow the *St. Louis* to make sure that no one tried to swim ashore. The liner was forced to turn back to Europe, its refugee passengers still aboard. European governmental hearts were a little softer and Great Britain, France, Belgium, and the Netherlands each agreed to take about a fourth of the passengers. Large numbers of them subsequently fell into the hands of the Nazis and perished, but some of the ship's passengers survived to observe the fiftieth anniversary of their rejection at a reunion in Miami.

In late 1938 Franklin Roosevelt did take one effective step by executive action: he "suggested" to Labor Secretary Perkins that the six-month visitor visas of "political" refugees be automatically extended and reextended for successive six-month periods as they ran out. This enabled about 15,000 persons to remain in the United States. Clearly, despite the president's 1941 claim, the vaunted "haven of refuge" did not function very well. But, it is important to note, perhaps 150,000 refugees, the overwhelming majority of them Jews, did manage to reach the United States before Pearl Harbor, a significantly larger number than was admitted by any other nation: many thousands of others could have been saved by a more resolute policy.

The Evolution of American Policy Toward Vietnamese Refugees

TRICIA SPRINGSTUBB

An inevitable consequence of war is the creation of refugees, as people are uprooted from their homes or forced to escape from battle-ravaged towns. Since World War II the U.S. government has implemented many policies to help wartime refugees, such as the Displaced Persons Act of 1948 and the Refugee Relief Act of 1953. After the end of the Vietnam War in 1975, the United States found itself facing an influx of tens of thousands of South Vietnamese refugees who were fleeing their country following the North Vietnamese takeover of South Vietnam.

In the following selection Tricia Springstubb examines the two major waves of Vietnamese refugees—the first group arriving in 1975, the second group two years later—entering the United States, and looks at how American policy toward these refugees changed during that time. Springstubb describes how the initial wave of refugees was brought to transition camps, where they were tested for job skills, taught English, and introduced to American culture and customs. The refugees remained in the camps until they had received security clearance, after which they could return to Vietnam, leave for another country, live on their own in America, or find an

Tricia Springstubb, "Welcome to Freedom Land," *Immigrants in America: The Vietnamese Americans*. San Diego: Lucent Books, 2002. Copyright © 2002 by Lucent Books, Inc. Reproduced by permission.

American family to sponsor them. She asserts that these camps succeeded in helping the Vietnamese refugees become permanent American citizens. However, Springstubb writes, the camps closed by the end of 1975, and so the U.S. government had to change its approach to the second wave of refugees. These refugees initially lived in crowded camps throughout Asia until the United States loosened its entry restrictions and passed the Refugee Act of 1980, which created the Office of Refugee Resettlement and made it easier for Vietnamese refugees to enter America. Springstubb is an author of fiction and nonfiction books for children, including Immigrants in America: The Vietnamese Americans, *from which the following article has been selected.*

Permanent resettlement [for Vietnamese refugees] was a long and complex process. Escape was only the beginning. Those who left in the first wave spent a brief time in Asian refugee camps before being transferred to one of four transitional camps hastily set up in the United States. After these transitional camps, their next step was to find an American sponsor who would help them with the huge tasks of finding work and housing.

For those who came in the second wave, the transition was even more difficult. Because the American camps were closed in 1976, these later immigrants skipped the transitional camps and were swept directly from their Asian camp experience into a new, alien culture.

Their journeys turned out to be far more treacherous than imagined. Confused, fearful about starting over, and grieving for their abandoned homeland, many clung to the promise of a new life in the United States—or Freedom Land, as some refugees dubbed it—as their only solid hope.

American Responsibility

The United States had numerous reasons for accepting Vietnamese immigrants. By 1975, American Vietnamese ties went back more than a decade. The American government and, in large part, the American public, acknowledged a moral responsibility to a people who had lost everything in a war fought alongside American troops.

Adding to this feeling of responsibility was the long-standing tradition of aiding those who turned to the United States for rescue and freedom. In a 1975 speech urging Congress to appropriate money for aid to the Vietnamese, House Judiciary Chairman Peter Rodino declared, "When this country forgets its immigrant heritage and turns its back on the oppressed and homeless, we will indeed have

Vietnamese refugees wait to board a military transport ship. Once in America, the refugees lived in transitional camps where they were taught English and introduced to American culture.

written finis [the end] to the American dream."

Furthermore, by 1975, most Vietnamese had some familiarity with American culture. They had met American soldiers. Many had worked with American businesspeople. They had been exposed to American magazines, newspapers, and radio. The glimpses they had had of life in the United States looked enviably glamorous and wealthy. A South Vietnamese schoolteacher who left soon after the fall of Saigon recalled her first impression on reaching her new country. "I was happy! America! It is just like heaven! Because people live here in freedom! You can go anywhere. You can live richer."

As a result of the responsibility Americans felt toward the Vietnamese, in April 1975 the U.S. government set up processing centers for those immigrants. These centers, or camps, served those immigrants deemed refugees—that is, people in need of political asylum, who were guaranteed entry into the United States. One of these camps was in the Philippines. Another, one of the largest and most well known, was located on the island of Guam, an American territory. Here Anderson Air Force Base, a facility abandoned since World War II, was hastily converted to temporary housing.

Refugees in Guam

Within days of the first arrivals, officials on Guam realized that far more Vietnamese than anticipated would need accommodation. A makeshift "tent city" was created. Here the weary refugees received medical care, clothing, and any other necessities they lacked. Some were reunited with family. Others tried to get information about family members from whom they had been separated.

The journey and plight of these first refugees was front-page news in the American media. *Time* magazine described the center at Guam:

> The mammoth refugee complex bulges with 40,000 people. . . . At night, strands of arc lights create hard

patches of brightness among the heavy canvas tents. The refugees leave urgent personal messages about themselves, in graffiti all around the camp—on the fences leading into the huts and immigration tents, on the sides of the shower stalls, even in spray paint across their tent flaps. Said one sign, 'TRAN THI HONG DA DI CALIFOR-NIA.' (TRAN THI HONG GONE TO CALIFORNIA.)

Tran Thi Hong was lucky. Many refugees spent a long time waiting in camps. Without connections, the necessary paperwork to go to America could drag on for months. In fact, the average refugee stay in a camp in Guam or the Philippines was nine months. After that, the immigrants were transferred to camps in the continental United States.

Transitional Camps

In the weeks after the fall of Saigon, the United States opened four transitional refugee camps on American soil. The first and largest was Camp Pendleton in southern California. The other three were Fort Chafee in Arkansas, Eglin Air Force Base in Florida, and Indiantown Gap in Pennsylvania. The camps were jointly run by the military, the government's Interagency Task Force on Indochina Refugees, and a wide range of volunteer organizations, which became known by the acronym Volags (Volunteer agencies). The Volags included among others the International Refugee Service, the YMCA, the Red Cross, and many church groups, among them the United Hebrew Immigrant Assistance Service, the Lutheran Immigration Service, and the U.S. Catholic Conference.

Upon arrival in the American camps, immigrants were interviewed and screened for security purposes, a daunting task for the officials involved. Julia Vadala Taft, who headed the Interagency Task Force, describes some of the obstacles.

> We had . . . to do security clearance [a background check to make sure the refugees were not a threat to American society]—we have a requirement in this country that if

you are being brought in or are allowed to come in, either as a parolee or a refugee, you have to get your security clearances. Well, come to find out that there were a lot of agencies involved in security clearances. . . . We [the Interagency Task Force] were finding that we weren't able to process people out of the camps for two or three weeks because the security clearance process was just a nightmare.

Adapting to American Life

Technicalities like this were common, and life in the American camps required a good deal of patience. Much of the immigrant's day was spent waiting in lines: for meals, for medical exams, for various forms of government processing, and for testing job skills, and the English language comprehension. Translators helped determine hometowns, age, and the makeup of large family groups. In addition, the immigrants were finger-printed by the Immigration and Naturalization Service and issued Social Security cards. During this time, families and individuals lived in large barracks or tents, which afforded little privacy. Still, adults and children alike were encouraged to attend classes, where they were instructed in English and introduced to American customs, and the plentiful food and clean water were a great improvement over the poorer conditions of most of the Asian camps.

Yet many immigrants, describing their experience in the transitional camp, reported feeling discontent with their idleness and were uneasy about taking assistance from the government. Although little work was expected of them, many were eager to contribute, volunteering as translators, typists, or even cooks. At Camp Pendleton, dubbed "Operation New Arrival," the food served by military chefs— hamburgers, hot dogs, and spaghetti—caused stomach ailments among the newcomers. The Americans tried to oblige the immigrants' tastes, but in at least one case, they needed help. A *Time* magazine reporter wrote, "The Army had been supplying soggily cooked rice, but finally asked for help in its kitchens. Said a mess sergeant, 'Come and show me how to cook it properly.' A score of Vietnamese women volunteered."

Adapting to their unfamiliar environment took place not only in the mess halls, but also in the immigrants' daily contact with the American lifestyle. Entertainment, for example, was plentiful. The immigrants played volleyball, soccer, and Ping Pong. Camp officials showed American movies and sponsored concerts of American music. For the children, watching television was a fascinating way to learn about their new culture. In addition, many younger refugees spent their free time with officials and with volunteers, getting to know their adopted country on a one-on-one basis.

The camps' mission was to help those who qualified make the transition from temporary refugee to immigrant. Once the Vietnamese had received their security clearance, refugees had four main routes to leaving the camps: repatriating to another country, returning to Vietnam, proving they were self-sufficient, and finding an American sponsor. Sponsorship ultimately became the route most Vietnamese took.

Sponsoring an immigrant family was a substantial undertaking. American volunteer sponsors pledged to provide food, clothing, and shelter until the family became self-supporting. In addition, sponsors agreed to help the adults find work, to enroll the children in school, and to be available in any way to assist adaptation to American daily life. Although the government gave limited financial assistance, most of the responsibility fell on the sponsor. . . .

The Camps Are Closed

The transitional camps had taken on an enormous task. At Camp Pendleton alone, more than 7 million meals were served, and 165 babies were born. Yet the chief focus of the camps had always been to move the Vietnamese out as quickly and as efficiently as possible. Julia Vadala Taft, director of the Interagency Task Force on Indochina Refugees, wanted all the camps to be closed by Christmas. In an interview published in a 1996 issue of *Vietnam* magazine, she remembered, "I wanted these people [the immigrants] to celebrate their very first American Christmas in their own homes. . . . That was the goal. We let the voluntary agencies know that this was something we wanted, and so we kept the pressure on them to speed up the processing." Taft's goal became reality. By December 20, 1975, all four camps had closed.

Although the camps were helpful in many ways, the brief period they operated limited what they could do. Those Vietnamese who spoke English and had the most marketable job skills, were the most easily placed with sponsors and left first. For the fishermen, farmers, and soldiers, as well as for those immigrants who spoke no English, finding a sponsor was more difficult. Furthermore, part of the government's resettlement strategy was to disperse the refugees all across the country, so no one geographic area would be saturated. Many Vietnamese, though, were reluctant to be sent places where they might be the only foreigners. Others were wary of being sponsored by churches other than their own religion. As months passed, pressure to close the camps forced some immigrants to accept sponsorships they would not have chosen on their own.

Despite these limitations, the four American camps did fulfill their mission of helping the Vietnamese make the transition from temporary refugee to permanent immigrant. Beginning in 1976, however, arriving Vietnamese no longer had this stepping stone. Instead, they plunged directly into American society.

Crowded Refugee Camps

The camps' closing was supposed to be the end of U.S. resettlement efforts. The American government hoped that the exodus from Vietnam was over, and that the aid program would be completed by 1977.

However, the end of the Vietnam War by no means meant the end of the departures. Boat people continued to arrive in Malaysia, Thailand, Indonesia, the Philippines, and Singapore, where they crowded into camps overseen by the United Nations. By 1979 these Asian countries were experiencing what some scholars call "compassion fatigue." The countries' limited resources were strained by the destitute who continued to arrive with no end in sight, and their citizens, many of whom were in need themselves, protested, saying the Vietnamese were not their problem. Furthermore, despite humanitarian efforts, conditions in most of the camps were woefully inadequate, and the wait to leave was very long.

One young Vietnamese man described his experience in Thai refugee camps:

> Khao I Dang, a refugee camp in Thai territory, was . . . crowded with more than a hundred thousand people living in terrible conditions with minimal food, medical services and shelter and no recreational or educational activities. . . . After eight months living in Khao I Dang, I was transferred to Chan Vu Ri camp [also in Thailand] to be interviewed for resettlement. Then came the day they announced the decision. Some were eligible to go directly to the United States because they had relatives there. The rest would be transferred again. . . . I was in the latter group. . . .

One reason for the seemingly endless wait was American immigration law. As of 1977 only three hundred Asian immigrants per month were allowed to enter the United States. That same year, though, the U.S. Immigration Service decided to admit Vietnamese under seventh preference visas—visas applied to people who were escaping communism, thus allowing a person to enter the United States for two years. After two years, the refugee was required to seek immigrant status, and, eventually, permanent residence.

The Vietnamese took advantage of this opportunity, and

by 1979 the numbers of refugees continued to grow. That year, the desperate plight of the boat people reached such proportions that the United States once again sent rescue ships to the South China Sea. World outcry against the immigrants' suffering pressured the Vietnamese government to agree to participate in the Orderly Departure Program, established under the jurisdiction of the United Nations High Commissioner for Refugees. This program enabled people to leave Vietnam legally, either to be reunited with family members or for other humanitarian reasons. Since 1979 more than 480,000 Vietnamese have legally entered the United States under the Orderly Departure Program.

In addition, in 1980 President Jimmy Carter pushed for the passage of the Refugee Act, a law aimed at reducing entry restrictions for the Vietnamese. This act created the Office of Refugee Resettlement, which administers programs and services for refugees within the United States. It also provided states with money to assist the new arrivals for thirty-six months, provided the states had a satisfactory plan for administering that assistance. This new legislation eased the way for tens of thousands more Vietnamese to come to America.

A Challenging Transition

Arrival in America was bittersweet. Forced to leave, unable to bring many possessions, the immigrants felt a mixture of joy and fear. For most, the questions they faced were challenging: Where would they live? How would they live? What did this new, alien country offer—and what would it ask of them?

If the Vietnamese were unclear about what to expect, so, too, were most Americans. The Vietnamese comprised the largest single refugee group ever to arrive in the United States within such a short span of time. Concern about their impact was widespread. A May 1975 nationwide Gallup Poll asked Americans whether evacuated South Vietnamese should be allowed to live in the United States. The majority of the respondants, 54 percent, said that they should not.

This opposition had many roots. For some Americans, involvement in Vietnam had been such a long, painful, ultimately humiliating experience that they wished to forget it. For others, bitter feelings against the "enemy" lingered, made all the stronger by ignorance about Vietnamese culture. The Buddhist religion, for example, was uncommon in the United States, and the Vietnamese language was a barrier. The Vietnamese were also seen as a potential drain on states' public assistance programs.

Recession-Bred Resentment

The greatest opposition, however, was the result of America's economic climate. In 1975 the United States had sunk into its worst recession in decades. Businesses shut down and many people lost their jobs; in 1975, almost 8 million Americans were unemployed. A growing imbalance of goods imported from Asia angered some citizens, who blamed foreigners for putting Americans out of work. With jobs at a premium, many Americans opposed allowing foreigners in to compete for those jobs. This resentment was generalized toward Vietnam.

A May 1975 *New York Times* article found that, in general, workers who were hardest hit by the recession were the ones most vocal in their opposition. In his article "Wide Hostility Found to Vietnamese Influx," reporter Douglas E. Kneeland wrote,

> Those interviewed in hard-pressed Detroit and Los Angeles, for example, tended to be harsh in their resentment of the newcomers. . . . "People are losing their cars, houses, jobs," said a 35-year-old black auto worker in Detroit. . . . "Let them stay there [Vietnam] until we do something for people here." Another worker commented, "This area is overcrowded now. I don't see why we should sacrifice our jobs and bring in more people. We are not obligated to police the whole world."

Some state governments also had reservations. California, for instance, the location of Camp Pendleton, was home to nearly 1 million unemployed workers. Anxious that California citizens not lose jobs to foreign workers, then Governor Edmund Brown demanded that any aid bill passed by Congress stipulate that jobs be provided first for Americans.

A Desire to Help

By no means was the reaction to the Vietnamese completely negative. Many Americans were willing to shoulder the considerable responsibility of sponsoring them. Others felt a moral responsibility because of the damage caused by the war. And still others saw offering asylum and help as part of the American tradition.

In his *New York Times* article, Kneeland also interviewed Robert D. Vilbiss, a salesman who had been out of work for six months. Despite his own shaky economic situation, Vilbiss felt the United States had an obligation to help the Vietnamese. He cited how the United States had assisted both Hungarians and Cubans who sought asylum when their countries were, like Vietnam, taken over by communism. "'We have received refugees from other countries seeking to get out,' he said. 'We . . . can't deny the same to the Vietnamese.'"

As the immigrants became part of American society, even more people began to adopt Vilbiss's view. Julia Vadala Taft, director of the Interagency Task Force, was well aware of the public's initial negative feelings and concern. Soon, though, she says that opinion began to change.

> As soon as the media got there [inside the camps] and started interviewing the families . . . the American people could see . . . that these are living human beings who had gone through [great suffering] and were here seeking freedom and respite and a new life. Well, those [media] stories changed public attitudes. . . . By the end of June [1975] public support began to pick up. The Volags had their sponsorship campaigns under way and thousands of sponsors were coming forward.

The immigrants themselves contributed to that change in public opinion. In fact, Taft says they played an invaluable role in changing their fate. "I give credit to the refugees. . . . [They] went to communities all over the country. They worked hard. They were dear people. They were appreciative. They sold themselves [made people like them] and they are still selling themselves today."

Immigration Needs to Be Capped to Protect the Environment

ROY BECK

Debates about immigration policy at the beginning of the twenty-first century often center around the impact that an increasing population is having on America's environment. In the following excerpt from a 2001 anthology on immigration, Roy Beck argues that if the United States is to protect the environment—and hence the quality of life for all Americans—then the government must set a strict cap on the number of immigrants it will allow into the country each year. According to Beck, this cap is 255,000. He still feels that this number is too high, as it will ensure further environmental destruction, but he concedes that a compromise is necessary. Beck is the author of The Case Against Immigration *and the executive director of NumbersUSA.com, a Web site that supports reducing legal and illegal immigration.*

The most important question for Washington is whether a continuing stream of foreign workers and dependents into the country over the next few years will make it more or less difficult to achieve the economic, social or environmental goals of the American people.

Roy Beck, *Blueprints for an Ideal Legal Immigration Policy*. Washington, DC: Center for Immigration Studies, 2001. Copyright © 2001 by the Center for Immigration Studies. Reproduced by permission.

In other words, for the first time in decades Washington should consider basing its immigration policy on how many immigrants the nation actually needs. Officials should start the process at the zero level and add only the numbers that actually will help the Americans reach their goals.

The idea of immigration actually having to serve the goals of the American people will be considered somehow selfish by some. But a first principle of democratic nations is that their governments set public policy based on the will of the people. A people can choose goals in all kinds of ways that affect their material prosperity, their social comfort and their humanitarian desires. The government's choices should reflect the needs and desires of the people of this nation.

Educational and Humanitarian Goals

In examining the research on a number of major societal concerns, I have concluded the following about optimum annual immigration levels:

American Need: Educational Quality, Optimum Immigration: up to 5,000. The worst education results in the country tend to be found in the school districts where most immigrants settle. That isn't necessarily the fault of the immigrants; many of the school districts were in bad shape before Congress began filling them with foreign students. But none of them has anything to gain by receiving another immigrant child. Congressional immigration policies may be at their cruelest in the way they diminish the chance that children of some of America's poorest families will gain at their schools the education, the imagination, and the motivation to work for their share of the American dream.

To the extent that the immigrant children in those districts might receive a significant boost from the work of an especially talented foreign educator, those needs should easily be met if we set aside 5,000 slots each year for foreign professionals with extraordinary skills.

Cutting off all other immigration flow would allow those

over-challenged, over-crowded districts to concentrate on educating the native and immigrant students at hand, instead of expending so much energy and money each year trying to accommodate additional students in an ever-expanding array of languages and cultures.

Until urban school districts no longer complain of being over-crowded or of having high dropout rates, any additional immigration is likely to be harmful.

American Need: Meeting Humanitarian Goals, Optimum Immigration: 15,000 to 50,000. Americans are an exceptionally generous people, especially in their private gifts to assist citizens of the developing countries. This is driven by a combination of religious, moral, and ethical impulses. I believe most Americans have an emotional or spiritual need to do their share in helping the tens of millions of refugees around the world. The numbers are so huge that one can make a case that it is unethical to spend any money on expensive resettlement of refugees in the United States when the same money would bring so much relief to so many more people in the camps and in assisting refugees to return home.

Nonetheless, the international community has a system for designating refugees who for political reason have virtually no chance of returning to their homelands—or who are in danger if they remain in camps. America's generally recognized fair share of those special needs refugees generally runs between 15,000 and 35,000 per year. Re-settling refugees who do not meet the special needs criteria not only needlessly squanders limited resources but can create incentives for people to recklessly leave their homes and recklessly resist homeland return efforts. Thoughtful and effective humanitarianism would limit refugee admissions to the fair share of internationally recognized special needs refugees.

Similar considerations should also apply to asylum requests. Permanent asylum should be granted only to those seekers who meet the international standard for fear of persecution and who prove that there is little likelihood they could ever return home. But there should be a second level of temporary asylum that allows the persecuted to stay in America while waiting out the troubles back home but which assures that the asylee will leave the United States once the war is over, the dictator is deposed, or some other needed change has occurred. . . .

Thoughtful humanitarianism would not extend beyond those two categories. It certainly would not extend to those who would come to increase their consumption of material goods, education or health care. With 4.6 billion people living in countries below the average income of Mexico, there can be no ethical justification for showering a tiny fraction of a percent of the world's needy with U.S. residency at the expense of vulnerable Americans instead of turning all such outward humanitarian attention to the billions of people left behind in the sending countries.

Environmental Issues

American Need: Taming Urban Sprawl and the Destruction of Open Spaces, Farmland, and Natural Habitat, Optimun Immigration: Zero. Americans are absolutely fed up with the sprawl, traffic, congestion, and disappearing open-space opportunities that are the result of adding 1 million people each year. While it theoretically is possible to create so much population growth without those negative societal trends, there are no examples in America of that having occurred. U.S. Census Bureau measurements of changes in urbanized areas indicate that around half of all sprawl is related to population growth. The Census Bureau also shows that most U.S. population growth is the result of recent federal immigration policies.

Until there is a national consensus that our cities no longer have a problem of sprawl, congestion, and disappearing open spaces, the optimum level of immigration would be zero until the U.S. population size is stabilized.

American Need: Meeting Environmental Goals, Optimum Immigration: Zero. In a country where nearly half the lakes and rivers do not meet clean water standards and where 40 percent of the citizens live in cities that can't meet clean air standards, anything that adds to the total number of Americans flushing toilets, riding in vehicles, and consuming electricity is anti-environment.

Under current American fertility which is just under replacement level, any immigration over zero during the next few decades will increase the size of the U.S. population and put the country further away from meeting its environmental goals.

It is possible that the current number of Americans could reduce their consumption enough to meet all environmental goals and still have room for more people. But until the American people elect a government to institute the regulations, the taxes, and the enforcement to ensure that consumption is sufficiently reduced, any federal policy that forces U.S. population growth is an anti-environmental policy.

The point here is not that immigrants cause environmental problems but that people cause environmental problems—and federal immigration policy adds millions of extra people each decade.

The optimum level of immigration would be zero until we have substantially met most of the environmental goals that have been set by elected representatives of the American people.

Marriage and Adoption Rights

American Need: Right of U.S. Citizens to Marry or Adopt Overseas, Optimum Immigration: Currently Around 200,000. The United States has a long tradition of allowing its citizens to adopt orphans from other countries and to marry people in other countries and immediately bring them to America. This is part of the fabric of generous individual liberties that Americans cherish. Before the federal government began its major increases in immigration numbers back in the 1960s, around 40,000 additional immigrants each year moved to the United States based on this right of marriage and adoption. But because of the explosion in immigration, America is filled with a huge pool of foreign-born citizens—and their children—who have a much higher proclivity toward marrying overseas. There has been no limit on how many foreign people can be married and adopted each year so that this category alone surpasses 200,000 a year, almost as large as the entire annual immigration flow in an average year during the country's first 200 years (1776–1976).

Although there should be increased efforts to reduce the thousands of immigrants each year who engage in marriage fraud, the optimum number for the sake of preserving this right of citizens should be the present number with the flexibility to go up or down depending on the demand.

Many people claim that this individual freedom to marry and adopt overseas extends to naturalized foreign-born citizens being allowed to send for their adult brothers, sisters and parents. This strains credulity. Except for the small fraction of the immigrant flow that is refugees, immigrants chose to separate from their families by coming here. Nobody forced them. If they have a passionate need to live near their relatives, they should move back. Americans commonly live 3,000 miles from their brothers, sisters and parents inside the United States. There is no legitimate American need for immigrants to nurture a never-ending chain of family migration by sending for close adult relatives who send for their close adult relatives until in-laws and distant cousins of the original immigrant are coming. . . .

Parents of immigrants are a somewhat more difficult question. But generous visitor visas could allow for extended visits that would afford more time together than is the case for large numbers of native-born American citizens and their parents. Also, an immigrant is free to move back home to care for a parent during a crisis.

A final family category to consider is the one containing

the spouses and minor children of immigrants who have green cards but who have not yet become citizens. There is quite a backlog right now because Congress has extended three amnesties to illegal aliens beginning in 1986. If a person becomes an immigrant through normal channels, he or she automatically can bring a spouse and minor children. But if an immigrant marries in another country before becoming a U.S. citizen, the spouse and children must wait. Currently, that backlog is whittled down each year. The surest solution to the backlog is for the immigrant to become a citizen. Still there may be reason to study this more to see if the backlog reduction numbers should be increased a bit.

Saving Jobs for Americans

American Need: Protection of Workers from Wage Depression, Optimum Immigration: Up to 5,000. No American wage earner benefits from having his or her elected officials import workers who may compete for the same jobs or help to depress wages. That is true whether the American workers is an unskilled lettuce picker, a slightly skilled chicken slaughterer, a skilled construction tradesman, or a college-educated engineer.

The recent spectacle of high government officials and major newspaper editorialists calling for increased immigration in order to hold down wages makes a mockery of the egalitarian ideals of this nation. Until recently, the primary answer to tight labor markets in this country has always been to increase productivity through innovation, invention and capital investment. That traditional style allowed wages to rise so that the vast majority of full-time working Americans could enjoy middle class lives of dignity.

Mass importation of foreign labor also violates American-style egalitarianism by creating vast underclass populations cast semi-permanently into the role of servants. Rising income disparity has always been the result of surges in immigration in this country.

Denying industries the immigrant workers they desire should not be a punitive measure. It is in the best interest of all Americans that our industries succeed—and, for that matter, that entrepreneurs and the owners of capital earn generous profits as they create jobs for the rest of us. The government should provide the industries the means to meet real short-term labor emergencies, as long as they do not impede efforts to train Americans to fill the needs later. Foreign workers given only temporary work visas, not by immigrants allowed to enter the United States for permanent residence, should fill neatly all skilled-job vacancies for which an American cannot be found. And temporary workers should be allowed into the country only after they have signed agreements of understanding that they will return to their home country at the end of the short time it may take to train enough Americans to take the jobs.

An allowance for 5,000 brilliant professionals would more than handle the number of scientists, professors, computer whizzes, and so forth who possess extraordinary genius and whom U.S. industries and universities want to steal from other countries each year.

The Optimum Level of Immigration

American Need: All of the Above, Overall Optimum Immigration: 100,000. The dilemma in setting the overall numbers is that the optimal numbers for various American needs clash with each other. The American needs to meet environmental goals and to combat sprawl are best met with zero immigration for awhile, but the American need to have the individual liberty to fall in love with anybody in the world and then bring that person to the United States as a bride or groom calls for at least 200,000 immigrants each year. The American need for economic justice in wages and for educational relief for kids in overcrowded, underfunded schools is best met with no more than 5,000 immigrants each year. But the American need to take up our fair share of helping special refugees calls for up to 50,000 a year.

If one left out the issue of overseas marriages and adoptions, one could argue for an optimum immigration level of 55,000 a year.

But in weighing all American needs together, one could make a claim for an immigration level of around 100,000. That represents a compromise between the marriage rights and all other matters affecting Americans' quality of life. Combined with government estimates that more than 200,000 illegal aliens permanently settle in the United States each year, an overall ceiling of 100,000 legal immigrants still would exceed out-migration each year and add significantly to U.S. population growth. And that would further aggravate efforts to improve education, environmental quality, wage fairness and quality of life issues like sprawl. But the level would be relatively mild compared with present conditions.

A Practical Number of Immigrants

Individual liberty often trumps all other needs in the American culture. The optimum immigration numbers noted above would require tens of thousands of citizens to get in a waiting line of perhaps years to marry overseas or to bring a spouse from overseas after marrying. I do not see any practical possibility for limiting the virtually unlimited right of citizens to marry anybody they choose, regardless of home country, and immediately bringing them to this country. I believe Americans will insist on that right even though only a tiny fraction of them—especially native-born ones—will ever even think about using that right. This is a democracy; if Americans are willing to subjugate many of their other needs and desires to this particular right that is their choice. It also is my reluctant preference.

Thus, my proposed numerical level of overall immigration would be 255,000. . . .

I picked the number based on 200,000 spouses and minor children of U.S. citizens, 5,000 world-class skilled workers and professionals and 50,000 refugees, asylees and nuclear family of permanent resident aliens. If the refugee and asylee admissions fall below 50,000 each year, the leftover green cards could go to reduce the backlog of spouses and minor children of immigrants who have not become citizens.

Since the citizens' spouses and minor children category would go up and down each year, my number really is not a rigid 255,000 but a formula that would currently produce a number like that. The formulas would be: 55,000 a year, plus an unlimited number of spouses and minor children of U.S. citizens.

Trends suggest that my number might rise fairly close to 300,000 before it began coming down strongly. But as the years progressed and we had fewer and fewer recent immigrants in the marrying pool, my overall number should in a decade or two move back to the traditional immigration average, and maybe eventually even toward the 100,000 optimum level.

I am not pleased with the number I have had to pick because it will lead—according to Census projections—to at least another 50 million Americans by mid-century and at current fertility rates won't stop pressuring urban sprawl, congestion and natural habitat destruction until the next century. If not for a federal government that has refused to look at the effect of overall immigration numbers while constantly making decisions that increased them for four decades, those of us who are Baby Boomers would have lived to see the fruits of a stable population. Now I have already lost the chance to live in a stable America, but I feel guilty about denying the opportunity to my great-grandchildren. I have picked an annual immigration number so high that it compromises their future, as well as every generation in between. But I have picked the best number that I believe is possible. All who pick higher numbers—or who refuse to pick a number at all—propose to only accelerate the future damage from massive additional population growth.

THE
HISTORY
OF
ISSUES

CHAPTER 3

Creating Immigration Quotas

Chapter Preface

Immigration is often seen as a social and political issue, but at its core it is about numbers: determining how many immigrants a country can absorb before unemployment soars due to increasing numbers of workers, and government services and natural resources reach their breaking points. Immigration policies have thus often included quotas that limit the number of immigrants allowed to enter from different countries. The experience of Chinese immigrants shows how economic and political factors can influence U.S. immigration quotas.

Chinese immigration to the United States began in the mid-nineteenth century, when gold was discovered in California. Like thousands of other people, these newcomers were eager to find riches in their new home. After the gold rush ended, Chinese immigrants, primarily men, continued to arrive in the American West to work on the transcontinental railroad.

When there were jobs available for the newly arrived Chinese, they were welcome to enter the United States. However, increased unemployment rates and other economic problems in the 1870s led to political animosity toward immigrants. In 1882 Congress passed the Chinese Exclusion Act, which suspended the immigration of Chinese laborers from China for ten years. The act was renewed in 1892 and again in 1902. Although not officially a quota, the Exclusion Act served a similar purpose by bringing Chinese immigration to a near standstill. In 1887 only 10 Chinese immigrated to the United States compared to 39,500 only five years earlier.

Quotas became part of American immigration policy in the 1920s, with the federal government establishing quotas in 1921 and 1924 based on earlier censuses. These quotas favored immigrants from western and northern Europe, with Asian immigration almost completely eliminated. As the Exclusion Act was still in place, the Chinese presence in America fell sharply in the first decades of the twentieth century; from 1908 to 1930, 72,796 Chinese departed while 48,482 arrived in America. In 1940 the number of foreign-born Chinese Americans had dropped to 31,687, barely half what it had been only thirty years earlier.

The year 1940 marked a low point for the number of Chinese in America, but events during the subsequent decade would shift policies in Chinese immigrants' favor. Just as the economic situation of post–Civil War America had led to restrictive policies, the political situation surrounding World War II proved a boon to the Chinese. With China an ally in the war, Congress repealed the Exclusion Act and allowed foreign-born Chinese to become American citizens. A quota was set; while it was a low number, with only 105 Chinese permitted to enter each year, it marked a sea change in the treatment of Chinese immigrants.

The level of immigration from China was finally equal to that of other nations' rates after the passage of the Immigration Act of 1965, which replaced country quotas with an overall quota. The act essentially placed immigrants from Asia on equal footing with those from more traditional sources of American immigration such as Europe and Latin America. Chinese immigrants now represent more than 4 percent of immigrants entering the United States.

Chinese immigrants are but one of the populations that have been affected by immigration quotas, but their experience highlights the ways in which economic, social, and political factors can determine the number of immigrants that are welcomed to the United States. In the following chapter the authors debate whether quotas are effective and necessary or if such policies are unfair.

The Immigration Act of 1924: Inventing National Origins

MAE M. NGAI

The United States has experienced several waves of immigration, including an influx of immigrants from Asia and southern and eastern Europe from the 1880s until the 1920s. Congress, fearing how these newcomers would impact the largely Protestant and western European–influenced American culture, began developing quotas to control the entrance of immigrants from "undesirable" nations. The first such quota was passed in 1921 and focused primarily on European immigration. The second quota established was the Immigration Act of 1924. It further limited the number of European immigrants allowed to enter the United States, particularly those from southern and eastern Europe, and barred Asians from becoming American citizens. In so doing the immigration act established national origins as being the central element of the U.S. quota system.

In the following selection, Mae M. Ngai explores the creation of quotas during the first quarter of the twentieth century. According to Ngai, politicians and demographers of that era considered U.S. census data to be proof that immigrants were overwhelming the United States. They also made popular the idea that race should be considered in forming immigration policies. Ngai concludes that congresspersons and other key federal figures relied on racist tenets to formulate quotas that stood for forty years, until the passage of the Im-

Mae M. Ngai, "The Architecture of Race in American Immigration Law: A Reexamination of the Immigration Act of 1924," *Journal of American History,* vol. 86, June 1999. Copyright © 1999 by the Organization of American Historians. Reproduced by permission.

migration Act of 1965. Ngai is an assistant professor of U.S. history at the University of Chicago.

This [viewpoint] argues that the Immigration Act of 1924 comprised a constellation of reconstructed racial categories, in which race and nationality—concepts that had been loosely conflated since the nineteenth century—disaggregated and realigned in new and uneven ways. At one level, the new immigration law differentiated Europeans according to nationality and ranked them in a hierarchy of desirability. At another level, the law constructed a white American race, in which persons of European descent shared a common whiteness that made them distinct from those deemed to be not white. Euro-Americans acquired both ethnicities—that is, nationality-based identities that were presumed to be transformable—and a racial identity based on whiteness that was presumed to be unchangeable. This distinction gave all Euro-Americans a stake in what [professor] Matthew Jacobson has called a "consanguine white race" and facilitated their Americanization. But, while Euro-Americans' ethnic and racial identities became uncoupled, non-European immigrants—among them Japanese, Chinese, Mexicans, and Filipinos—acquired ethnic and racial identities that were one and the same. The racialization of the latter groups' national origins rendered them unalterably foreign and unassimilable to the nation. The Immigration Act of 1924 thus established legal foundations for social processes that would unfold over the next several decades, processes that historians have called, for European immigrants, "becoming American" (or, more precisely, white Americans), while casting Mexicans as illegal aliens and foredooming Asians to permanent foreignness.

Drawing upon [professors] Michael Omi and Howard Winant's concept of racial formation, which they define as "the sociohistorical process by which racial categories are created, inhabited, transformed, and destroyed," this [viewpoint] seeks to understand the role of immigration law and policy in the production of official knowledges of race and nationality. The [viewpoint] . . . analyzes the invention of "national origins," which applied mostly to Europeans while distinguishing Europeans from non-Europeans, and the attendant process by which immigration quotas were determined as practical policy. . . .

This analysis of the Immigration Act of 1924 suggests that immigration law and policy were deeply implicated in a broader racial and ethnic remapping of the nation during the 1920s, a remapping that took place in mutually constituting realms of demography, economics, and law. It involved, in addition to changes in immigration patterns and policy, the migration of African Americans from the South to northern cities and the legal justification for de facto segregation in the North, and the completion of the legal process of forced assimilation of American Indians.

Calculating Quotas

If the quota system went into effect without the unqualified confidence of its authors, the project had been marked by doubt from the beginning. Census and immigration records, upon which the Quota Board relied in making its calculations, were woefully incomplete. The census of 1790, the nation's first, did not include information about national origin or ancestry. The census did not differentiate the foreign-born until 1850 and did not identify the places of birth of parents of the native-born until 1890. Immigration was unrecorded before 1820 and not classified according to origin until 1899, when it was arranged, not by politically defined nation-states, but according to a taxonomy called "races and peoples." Emigration was not recorded until 1907. To complicate things further, many boundaries in Europe changed after World War I, requiring a translation of political geography to reattribute origins and allocate quotas according to the world in 1920.

To calculate the quotas, the Quota Board first had to conceptualize the categories that constituted the system. "National origin," "native stock," "nationality," and other categories in the system were not natural units of classification; they were constructed according to certain social values and political judgments. Race, never explicitly mentioned in the statute, nevertheless entered the calculus and subverted the conceptual foundations of the system in myriad ways. For example, the board defined "native stock," not as persons born in the United States, but as persons who descended from the white population of the United States in 1790. It defined "foreign stock" as the descendants of all whites who immigrated to the United States after 1790.

The law defined "nationality" according to country of birth. But that definition did not apply to the American nationality. The statute excluded non-European peoples residing in the United States from the population universe governing the quotas. The law stipulated that "'inhabitants in continental United States in 1920' does not include (1) immigrants from the [Western Hemisphere] or their descendants, (2) aliens ineligible to citizenship or their descendants, (3) the descendants of slave immigrants, or (4) the descendants of the American aborigines."

The Quota Board used census race categories to make its calculations. It subtracted from the total United States population all blacks and mulattoes, eliding the difference between the "descendants of slave immigrants" and the descendants of free Negroes and voluntary immigrants from Africa. It also discounted all Chinese, Japanese, and South Asians as persons "ineligible to citizenship," including descendants of such people with American citizenship by native birth. Finally, it left out the populations of Hawaii, Puerto Rico, and Alaska, which American immigration law governed and whose native-born inhabitants were United States citizens.

The Meaning of Nationality

In other words, to the extent that the "inhabitants in continental United States in 1920" constituted a legal representation of the American nation, the law excised all nonwhite, non-European peoples from that vision, erasing them from the American nationality. The practical consequence of those erasures is clear enough. In 1920 African Americans accounted for approximately 9 percent of the total United States population. Had they been included in the base population governing the quotas, the African nations from which they originated would have received 9 percent of the total immigration quota, resulting in 13,000 fewer slots for the European nations.

Race altered the meaning of nationality in other ways as well. Formally, the quota system encompassed all countries in the world outside the Western Hemisphere. China, Japan, India, and Siam each received the minimum quota of 100, but the law excluded the native citizens of those countries from immigration because they were deemed to be racially ineligible to citizenship. Thus Congress created the oddity of immigration quotas for non-Chinese persons from China, non-Japanese persons from Japan, non-Indian persons from India, and so on. The independent African nations of Ethiopia, Liberia, and South Africa received quotas of 100 each. Because the latter was a white settler country, this amounted to a concession of 200 immigration slots for black Africans. European mandates and protectorates in Africa, the Near East, and the Far East—for example, Tanganyika, Cameroon, Palestine, New Guinea—had their own quotas, which in practice served to increase the quotas of Great Britain, France, and Belgium, the nations with the largest colonial empires.

Thus while the national origins quota system was intended principally to restrict immigration from the nations of southern and eastern Europe and used the notion of national origins to justify discrimination against immigration from those nations, it did more than divide Europe. It also divided Europe from the non-European world. It defined the world formally by country and nationality but also by race, distinguishing between white persons from white countries and so-called colored races, whose members were imagined as having no countries of origin. This cross-cutting taxonomy was starkly presented in a table prepared by John Trevor, an advocate of immigration restriction and the chief lobbyist for a coalition of patriotic societies, on the national origins of the American people in 1924, which listed under the column "Country of Origin" fifty-three countries (from Australia to Yugoslavia) and five "colored races" (black, mulatto, Chinese, Japanese, and Indian).

Like most of their contemporaries, members of Congress and the Quota Board[1] treated race as evidence in itself of differences that they presumed were natural. Few, if any, doubted that the Census Bureau's categories of race were objective divisions of objective reality. Such confidence evinced the strength of race thinking generally as well as the progressivist faith in science, in this case, the sciences of demography and statistics. Indeed, few people doubted the census at all. The census carried the weight of official statistics; its power lay in the seeming objectivity of numbers and in its formalization of racial categories. Census data gave the quotas an imprimatur that was nearly unimpeachable. The census was invoked with remarkable authority, as when, during the floor debate in the House in 1924, Rep. William Vaile retorted to an opponent of the national origins principle, "Then the gentleman does not agree with the Census!"

The Work of Francis A. Walker

Demography, and the census itself, far from being the simple quantification of material reality, grew in the late nineteenth and early twentieth centuries as a language for interpreting the social world. As the historian Margo Anderson observes, census classifications that defined urban and rural populations, social and economic classes,

1. The Quota Board was a committee comprised of members of the State, Commerce, and Labor Departments.

and racial groups created a vocabulary for public discourse on the great social changes taking place in the United States—industrialization, urban growth, and, of course, immigration. In fact, the census was the favored form of scientific evidence cited by restrictionists and nativists during this period. That practice began with census officials. Francis A. Walker, the superintendent of the 1870 and 1880 censuses, was president of the Massachusetts Institute of Technology (MIT) and a brilliant scholar in the new field of statistics. He was also an ardent nativist and social Darwinist who believed immigrants from Italy, Hungary, Austria, and Russia were "vast masses of peasantry, degraded below our utmost conceptions . . . beaten men from beaten races, representing the worst failures in the struggle for existence."

Analyzing census data, Walker developed the theory that by the 1880s immigration was retarding the natural birthrate of Americans, which he lauded as the highest in the world since the founding of the Republic and as evidence of the nation's greatness. Because immigrants crowded native-born Americans from unskilled jobs, Walker theorized, the latter adjusted to their limited job opportunities by having fewer children. He considered immigration a "shock" to the principle of natural population increase.

His theory rested on the assumption that the nation possessed a natural character and teleology, to which immigration was external and unnatural. That assumption resonated with conventional views about America's providential mission and the general march of progress. Yet, it was rooted in a profoundly conservative viewpoint that the composition of the American nation should never change. Few people during the 1920s understood, much less accepted, the view of the philosopher Horace Kallen, an advocate of cultural pluralism, that the English had settled the North American Atlantic seaboard, not as a result of prompting from Providence, but as an accident of history.

Francis Walker's theory of the declining native birthrate

and the census data upon which it was based became the foundation for the restrictionists' claim that immigration threatened to overwhelm the American nation. It anchored Madison Grant's[2] thesis that the great Nordic race was in danger of extinction. Paraphrasing Walker, Grant warned that upward mobility on the part of native workers was a form of race suicide. "A race that refuses to do manual work and seeks 'white collar' jobs," he said, "is doomed through its falling birth rate to replacement by the lower races or classes. In other words, the introduction of immigrants as lowly laborers means a replacement of race." Similarly, a 1922 publication by the Commonwealth Club of California, a civic forum devoted to discussion of policy issues, on "Immigration and Population" carried the subtitle, "The Census Returns Prove That Immigration in the Past Century Did Not Increase the Population, but Merely Replaced One Race Stock by Another."

Scientific Racism

Like Francis Walker, Joseph Hill also came from an elite, old-line New England family. The son of a minister and a cousin of Henry Adams, he graduated from Phillips Exeter Academy and Harvard College (as had his father and grandfather) and received his Ph.D. at the University of Halle, Germany. Although Hill began his tenure at the Census Bureau in 1899, two years after Walker's death, he held many of the same views. In 1910, using previously unpublished and untabulated census data, Hill contributed to the Dillingham Commission's study of immigration two monographs that were of great importance to the restrictionist movement. The first study analyzed occupational distribution by nativity; the second determined differentials in fecundity between the foreign-born, the native-born of foreign-born parents, and the native-born of native parents. Not coincidentally, these

2. Grant was a lawyer and eugenicist who helped shape America's immigration policies in the 1920s.

studies provided additional empirical evidence for Francis Walker's theory of the retarded native birthrate.

Since the mid-nineteenth century, scientific race theory had revolved around efforts to develop systems of racial classification and typology. In this vein, Hill strove for ever more precise categories of classification and comparisons of type. He added new questions to the census in 1910 and 1920 in the hope of elucidating differences in race and nationality in increasing detail. Hill restored the "mulatto" race category (which had been eliminated in the 1900 census) as well as questions to ascertain literacy, ability to speak English, mother tongue, number of children born and living, and length of time in the United States. He was particularly interested in creating indices to gauge assimilation, and he presented data in tables that made racial comparisons convenient.

In a sense, demographic data were to twentieth-century racists what craniometric data had been to race scientists during the nineteenth. Like the phrenologists who preceded them, the eugenicists worked backward from classifications they defined *a priori* and declared a causal relationship between the data and race. Instead of measuring skulls, they counted inmates in state institutions. If statistics showed that immigrants were less healthy, less educated, and poorer than native-born Americans, that was deemed evidence of the immigrants' inferior physical constitution, intelligence, and ambition.

Unlike Francis Walker, Joseph Hill did not aggressively campaign for restriction. He endorsed the national origins principle in a restrained way and otherwise scrupulously avoided taking political positions. Yet, like all scientists, he brought his own political views and values to his work—to the questions he asked, to the ways in which he classified data, and to the interpretations he drew from the data. In Hill's case, those politics had guided a proliferation of census data on the foreign-born that served the nativist movement.

That is not to say that Hill's work was unscientific or unprofessional. To the contrary, he was a serious professional who worked according to the established methods and disciplinary requirements of his field. As [historian] Nancy Stepan has pointed out, scientific racism's power lay, in large part, in its adherence to scientific methodology and disciplinary standards. If race science were merely pseudoscience, it would have had far less currency.

In fact, Hill agonized over the methodological problems in determining national origins. One of the most serious problems he confronted was the lack of reliable information about the national origins of the white native-stock population. Hill deduced that roughly half the white population in 1920 consisted of descendants from the original colonial population, but the census of 1790 did not record data on place of birth. A study conducted by the Census Bureau in 1909, *A Century of Population Growth*, classified the population of 1790 according to country of origin by analyzing the surnames of the heads of households recorded in the census. The study found 87 percent of the population to be English. Independent scholars believed the report was inaccurate, however, because it failed to recognize that some names were common to more than one country and that many Irish and German names had been anglicized. It omitted Scandinavians from the national composition altogether. Hill too believed the report was "of questionable value."

Problematic Calculations

Nevertheless, Hill decided to use *A Century of Population Growth* because no other data existed. But after protests mounted from groups of Irish, German, and Scandinavian Americans, he realized that the flawed report endangered the credibility of the entire exercise. With the help of a $10,000 grant from the American Council of Learned Societies, Hill enlisted Howard Barker, a genealogist, and Marcus Hansen, an immigration historian, to determine the national origins of the white population in 1790. Their conclusions, based on a more sophisticated method of analyzing surnames and reported to the Quota Board in 1928, adjusted the allocations of origins of the colonial stock considerably. Great Britain and Northern Ireland's share fell from 82 percent to 67 percent of the total, reducing its quota by 10,000.

Assuming that Barker and Hansen discerned the national origins of the population in 1790 with fair accuracy, determining the national origins of the American population from that base, following their descendants forward in time from 1790 to 1920, was an entirely different matter. The methodology employed by the Quota Board analyzed the population in terms of numerical equivalents, not actual persons. Hill explained that the Quota Board could not "classify people into so many distinct groups of individual persons, each group representing the number of individual persons descending from a particular country." He continued,

> Even if we had complete genealogical records that would not be possible because there has been a great mixture of nationalities through inter-marriage since this country was first settled. So when the law speaks of the number of inhabitants having a particular national origin, the inhabitant must be looked upon as a unit of measure rather than a distinct person. That is to say, if we have, for example, four people each of whom had three English grandparents and one German grandparent, . . . we have the equivalent of three English inhabitants and one German inhabitant.

Using numerical equivalents may have been the only available statistical method, but it revealed the fundamental problem of the whole project. The method treated national identities as immutable and transhistorical, passed down through generations without change. The Quota Board assumed that even if nationalities combined through intermarriage, they did not mix but remained in descendants as discrete, unalloyed parts that could be tallied as fractional equivalents. . . .

The Quota Board also ignored intermarriage between Euro-Americans and both African Americans and Native American Indians, never problematizing the effect of miscegenation on the "origins" of the white population. That was because no conceptual space for such consideration existed in the absolutism of American racial construction. Thus, even as the board proceeded from an assumption that all bloodlines were inviolate, it conceptualized national origin and race in fundamentally different ways.

Even when considered on its own terms, the task of calculating national origins was beset by methodological problems. The Quota Board had to make assumptions to fill the gaps in the data. Hill acknowledged that his computations involved "rather arbitrary assumptions," some of which did "violence to the facts." The most serious—and surprising, in light of Hill's long-standing interest in immigrant fecundity—was his decision to apply the same rate of natural increase to all national groups. Hill also weighted the population figures for each decade, giving each earlier decade greater numerical importance than the succeeding one, to allow for a larger proportion of descendants from earlier immigrants. The net result of these assumptions tilted the numbers toward the northern European nationalities.

Hill himself expressed concern that the entire exercise rested on so many assumptions that the conclusions might not be viable. Ultimately, Hill rationalized, arguing that errors in the process would not significantly affect the outcome. Because the law assigned one quota slot for each 600 people in the 1920 population, Hill said, a deviation of 60,000 in the population of any nationality would alter its quota by only 100. A more honest inquiry might have concluded that determining the national origins of the American people was theoretically suspect and methodologically impossible. But, once President Hoover promulgated the quotas in 1929, the "national origins" of the American people, and the racial hierarchies embedded in them, assumed the prestige of law and the mantle of fact. . . .

The Legacy of Racialization

Lawmakers had invoked anthropology and scientific racism to create immigration restriction based on national origin, but it fell to civil servants in the executive branch to devise actual categories of identity for purposes of regulating immigration and immigrants. Indeed, the enumeration and classification of the American people enabled such regulation. As [professor] Vicente Rafael has suggested, the value of such population schedules to the modern state lay in their "rendering visible the entire field of [state] intervention." Thus the invention of national origins and unassimilable races was as much a project of state building as it was one of ideology. Indeed, if World War I marked the end of the "long nineteenth century," the United States emerged during the 1920s in full modern dress. Key to its modern persona was a comprehensive race policy that was unprecedented in scope and embedded in the law and in official practices at the federal level. Immigration policy and its specific constructions of race enabled the state to demarcate and police both the external boundaries and the internal spaces of the nation.

Congress, the Quota Board, the Supreme Court, and the Immigration Service produced and reproduced categories of difference that turned on both nationality and race, reclassifying Americans as racialized subjects simultaneously along both axes. The Immigration Act of 1924 contributed to the racialization of immigrant groups around notions of whiteness, permanent foreignness, and illegality—categories of difference that have outlived the racial categories created by eugenics and post–World War I nativism. Those legacies remain with us to this day, as [professor] Lisa Lowe has described, in "racial formations that are the material trace of history."

Quotas Are Racially Discriminatory

ROBERT H. CLANCY

Prior to the 1880s, most immigration into the United States came from western and northern European nations. However, political changes in southern and eastern Europe prompted a greater influx of immigrants from those regions in the late nineteenth and early twentieth centuries. Concerns about the ways these immigrants were changing the demographics of the United States prompted the U.S. government to establish immigration quotas; the first such quota, which restricted European immigration, was approved by Congress in 1921.

In the following selection Robert H. Clancy, a Republican congressman from Detroit, argues against the 1924 Johnson-Reed Act, which set restrictive immigration quotas and revised the Quota Act of 1921. He contends that the act is racially discriminatory because it is biased against southern and eastern Europeans. According to Clancy, Italian, Jewish, and Polish immigrants have proven themselves to be industrious, patriotic, and worthy of being welcomed into the United States. He argues that the act is un-American because all Americans have foreign ancestors. Clancy believes that its passage will worsen racial hatred and antagonism. The act passed overwhelmingly, with only six votes cast against it.

S ince the foundations of the American commonwealth were laid in colonial times over 300 years ago, vigorous complaint and more or less bitter persecution have been

Robert H. Clancy, address to the U.S. Congress, Washington, DC, April 8, 1924.

aimed at newcomers to our shores. Also the congressional reports of about 1840 are full of abuse of English, Scotch, Welsh immigrants as paupers, criminals, and so forth.

Old citizens in Detroit of Irish and German descent have told me of the fierce tirades and propaganda directed against the great waves of Irish and Germans who came over from 1840 on for a few decades to escape civil, racial, and religious persecution in their native lands.

The "Know-Nothings," lineal ancestors of the Ku-Klux Klan, bitterly denounced the Irish and Germans as mongrels, scum, foreigners, and a menace to our institutions, much as other great branches of the Caucasian race of glorious history and antecedents are berated to-day. All are riff-raff, unassimilables, "foreign devils," swine not fit to associate with the great chosen people—a form of national pride and hallucination as old as the division of races and nations.

The Fearful Fallacy

But to-day it is the Italians, Spanish, Poles, Jews, Greeks, Russians, Balkanians, and so forth, who are the racial lepers. And it is eminently fitting and proper that so many Members of this House [of Representatives] with names as Irish as Paddy's pig, are taking the floor these days to attack once more as their kind has attacked for seven bloody centuries the fearful fallacy of chosen peoples and inferior peoples. The fearful fallacy is that one is made to rule and the other to be abominated. . . .

In this bill [the Johnson-Reed Act] we find racial discrimination at its worst—a deliberate attempt to go back 84 years in our census taken every 10 years so that a blow may be aimed at peoples of eastern and southern Europe, particularly at our recent allies in the Great War [World War I]—Poland and Italy.

Targeting Jews and Italians

Of course the Jews too are aimed at, not directly, because they have no country in Europe they can call their own, but they are set down among the inferior peoples. Much of the animus against Poland and Russia, old and new, with the countries that have arisen from the ruins of the dead Czar's European dominions, is directed against the Jew.

We have many American citizens of Jewish descent in Detroit, tens of thousands of them—active in every profession and every walk of life. They are particularly active in charities and merchandising. One of our greatest judges, if not the greatest, is a Jew [Louis Brandeis]. Surely no fair-minded person with a knowledge of the facts can say the Jews or Detroit are a menace to the city's or the country's well-being. . . .

Forty or fifty thousand Italian-Americans live in my district in Detroit. They are found in all walks and classes of life—common hard labor, the trades, business, law, medicine, dentistry, art, literature, banking, and so forth.

They rapidly become Americanized, build homes, and make themselves into good citizens. They brought hardihood, physique, hope, and good humor with them from their outdoor life in Sunny Italy, and they bear up under the terrific strain of life and work in busy Detroit.

One finds them by thousands digging streets, sewers, and building foundations, and in the automobile and iron and steel fabric factories of various sorts. They do the hard work that the native-born American dislikes. Rapidly they rise in life and join the so-called middle and upper classes. . . .

The Italian-Americans of Detroit played a glorious part in the Great War. They showed themselves as patriotic as the native born in offering the supreme sacrifice.

In all, I am informed, over 300,000 Italian-speaking soldiers enlisted in the American Army, almost 10 percent of our total fighting force. Italians formed about 4 percent of the population of the United States and they formed 10 percent of the American military force. Their casualties were 12 percent. . . .

I wish to take the liberty of informing the House that from my personal knowledge and observation of tens of thousands of Polish-Americans living in my district in Detroit that their Americanism and patriotism are unassailable from any fair or just standpoint.

The Polish-Americans are as industrious and as frugal and as loyal to our institutions as any class of people who have come to the shores of this country in the past 300 years. They are essentially home builders, and they have come to this country to stay. They learn the English language as quickly as possible, and take pride in the rapidity with which they become assimilated and adopt our institutions.

Figures available to all show that in Detroit in the World War the proportion of American volunteers of Polish blood

The Johnson-Reed Act of 1924 discriminated against immigrants from certain parts of Europe, such as this family from Italy.

was greater than the proportion of Americans of any other racial descent. . . .

Polish-Americans do not merit slander nor defamation. If not granted charitable or sympathetic judgment, they are at least entitled to justice and to the high place they have won in American and European history and citizenship.

The force behind the Johnson bill and some of its champions in Congress charge that opposition to the racial discrimination feature of the 1800 quota basis arises from "foreign blocs." They would give the impression that 100 percent Americans are for it and that the sympathies of its opponents are of the "foreign-bloc" variety, and bear stigma of being "hyphenates." I meet that challenge willingly. I feel my Americanism will stand any test.

Every American Has Foreign Ancestors

The foreign born of my district writhe under the charge of being called "hyphenates." The people of my own family were all hyphenates—English-Americans, German-Americans, Irish-Americans. They began to come in the first ship or so after the *Mayflower*. But they did not come too early to miss the charge of anti-Americanism. Roger Williams was driven out of the Puritan colony of Salem to die in the wilderness because he objected "violently" to blue laws and the burning or hanging of rheumatic old women on witchcraft charges. He would not "assimilate" and was "a grave menace to American Institutions and democratic government." My family put 11 men and boys into the Revolutionary War, and I am sure they and their women and children did not suffer so bitterly and sacrifice until it hurt to establish the autocracy of bigotry and intolerance which exists in many quarters to-day in this country. Some of these men and boys shed their blood and left their bodies to rot on American battle fields. To me real Americanism and the American flag are the product of the blood of men and of the tears of women and children of a different type than the rampant "Americanizers" of to-day.

My mother's father fought in the Civil War, leaving his six small children in Detroit when he marched away to the southern battle fields to fight against racial distinctions and protect his country.

My mother's little brother, about 14 years old, . . . fired by the traditions of his family, plodded off to the battle fields to do his bit. He aspired to be a drummer boy and inspire the men in battle, but he was found too small to carry a drum and was put at the ignominious task of driving army mules, hauling cannons and wagons.

I learned more of the spirit of American history at my mother's knee than I ever learned in my four years of high school study of American history and in my five and a half years of study at the great University of Michigan.

All that study convinces me that the racial discriminations of this bill are un-American. . . .

It must never be forgotten also that the Johnson bill, although it claims to favor the northern and western European peoples only, does so on a basis of comparison with the southern and western European peoples. The Johnson bill cuts down materially the number of immigrants allowed to come from northern and western Europe, the so-called Nordic peoples. . . .

I can not stultify myself by voting for the present bill and overwhelm my country with racial hatreds and racial lines and antagonisms drawn even tighter than they are to-day.

Immigration Quotas Are Unfair to Europeans Fleeing Communism

HARRY S. TRUMAN

*During the late 1940s and early 1950s, the "Red Scare"
reached its height in the United States. Many citizens and politicians, most notably Senator Joseph McCarthy, alleged that
dozens of government employees held Communist beliefs and
thus posed a threat to national security. Meanwhile, the Communist nations of the Soviet Union and China were dominat-
ing American foreign policy concerns. The Soviet domination
of eastern Europe had caused the nations in that region to fall
to communism, prompting huge numbers of eastern Europeans—who possibly held dangerous political views—to flee
to America. It was in this environment that the Immigration
and Nationality Act of 1952, also known as the McCarran-
Walter Immigration Act, was approved by Congress.*

*In the following selection Harry S. Truman, the thirty-third
president of the United States, explains why he decided to
veto the Immigration and Nationality Act of 1952. In his statement, written on June 25, 1952, the president asserts that
while U.S. immigration laws need to be reformed and mod-
ernized, the bill is the wrong solution. He criticizes the bill's
retention of the 1924 quota system, contending that it intentionally discriminates against immigrants from southern and*

Harry S. Truman, "Veto of Bill to Revise the Laws Relating to Immigration, Naturalization, and Nationality," June 25, 1952.

eastern Europe. According to the president, the United States should welcome immigrants who are trying to flee Communist eastern Europe as well as immigrants from southern European nations that have proven to be valuable military allies. Truman also charges that the act is biased against Asian immigrants, although he acknowledges that certain provisions of the bill would benefit immigrants from that region. Truman's veto was overturned by Congress, and the bill was enacted two days after the veto was issued.

To the House of Representatives:
    I return herewith, without my approval, H.R. 5678, the proposed Immigration and Nationality Act.

In outlining my objections to this bill, I want to make it clear that it contains certain provisions that meet with my approval. This is a long and complex piece of legislation. It has 164 separate sections, some with more than 40 subdivisions. It presents a difficult problem of weighing the good against the bad, and arriving at a judgment on the whole.

H.R. 5678 is an omnibus bill which would revise and codify all of our laws relating to immigration, naturalization, and nationality.

A Step Backward

A general revision and modernization of these laws unquestionably is needed and long overdue, particularly with respect to immigration. But this bill would not provide us with an immigration policy adequate for the present world situation. Indeed, the bill, taking all its provisions together, would be a step backward and not a step forward. In view of the crying need for reform in the field of immigration, I deeply regret that I am unable to approve H.R. 5678.

In recent years, our immigration policy has become a matter of major national concern. Long dormant questions about the effect of our immigration laws now assume first rate importance. What we do in the field of immigration and naturalization is vital to the continued growth and internal development of the United States—to the economic and social strength of our country—which is the core of the defense of the free world. Our immigration policy is equally, if not more important to the conduct of our foreign relations and to our responsibilities of moral leadership in the struggle for world peace.

In one respect, this bill recognizes the great international significance of our immigration and naturalization policy, and takes a step to improve existing laws. All racial bars to naturalization would be removed, and at least some minimum immigration quota would be afforded to each of the free nations of Asia.

I have long urged that racial or national barriers to naturalization be abolished. This was one of the recommendations in my civil rights message to the Congress on February 2, 1948. On February 19, 1951, the House of Representatives unanimously passed a bill to carry it out.

The Flaws Outweigh the Improvements

But now this most desirable provision comes before me embedded in a mass of legislation which would perpetuate injustices of long standing against many other nations of the world, hamper the efforts we are making to rally the men of East and West alike to the cause of freedom, and intensify the repressive and inhumane aspects of our immigration procedures. The price is too high, and in good conscience I cannot agree to pay it.

I want all our residents of Japanese ancestry, and all our friends throughout the far East, to understand this point clearly. I cannot take the step I would like to take, and strike down the bars that prejudice has erected against them, without, at the same time, establishing new discriminations against the peoples of Asia and approving harsh and repressive measures directed at all who seek a new life within our boundaries. I am sure that with a little more time and a little more discussion in this country the public conscience and the good sense of the American people will assert themselves, and we shall be in a position to enact an immigration and naturalization policy that will be fair to all. In addition to removing racial bars to naturalization, the bill would permit American women citizens to bring their alien husbands to this country as non-quota immigrants, and enable alien husbands of resident women aliens to come in under the quota in a preferred status. These provisions would be a step toward preserving the integrity of the family under our immigration laws, and are clearly desirable.

The bill would also relieve transportation companies of some of the unjustified burdens and penalties now imposed upon them. In particular, it would put an end to the archaic requirement that carriers pay the expenses of aliens detained at the port of entry, even though such aliens have arrived with proper travel documents.

But these few improvements are heavily outweighed by other provisions of the bill which retain existing defects in our laws, and add many undesirable new features.

An Out-of-Date Quota System

The bill would continue, practically without change, the national origins quota system, which was enacted into law in 1924, and put into effect in 1929. This quota system—always based upon assumptions at variance with our American ideals—is long since out of date and more than ever unrealistic in the face of present world conditions.

This system hinders us in dealing with current immigration problems, and is a constant handicap in the conduct of our foreign relations. As I stated in my message to Congress on March 24, 1952, on the need for an emergency program of immigration from Europe, "Our present quota system is not only inadequate to most present emergency needs, it is also an obstacle to the development of an enlightened and satisfactory immigration policy for the long-run future."

The inadequacy of the present quota system has been demonstrated since the end of the war, when we were compelled to resort to emergency legislation to admit displaced persons. If the quota system remains unchanged, we shall be compelled to resort to similar emergency legislation again, in order to admit any substantial portion of the refugees from communism or the victims of overcrowding in Europe.

With the idea of quotas in general there is no quarrel. Some numerical limitation must be set, so that immigration will be within our capacity to absorb. But the overall limitation of numbers imposed by the national origins quota system is too small for our needs today, and the country by country limitations create a pattern that is insulting to large numbers of our finest citizens, irritating to our allies abroad, and foreign to our purposes and ideals.

Harry S. Truman

The overall quota limitation, under the law of 1924, restricted annual immigration to approximately 150,000. This was about one-seventh of one percent of our total population in 1920. Taking into account the growth in population since 1920, the law now allows us but one-tenth of one percent of our total population. And since the largest national quotas are only partly used, the number actually coming in has been in the neighborhood of one-fifteenth of one percent. This is far less than we must have in the years ahead to keep up with the growing needs of the Nation for manpower to maintain the strength and vigor of our economy.

Discrimination Against Southern and Eastern Europeans

The greatest vice of the present quota system, however, is that it discriminates, deliberately and intentionally, against many of the peoples of the world. The purpose behind it was to cut down and virtually eliminate immigration to this country from Southern and Eastern Europe. A theory was invented to rationalize this objective. The theory was that in order to be readily assimilable, European immigrants should be admitted in proportion to the numbers of persons of their respective national stocks already here as shown by the census of 1920. Since Americans of English, Irish and German descent were most numerous, immigrants of those three nationalities got the lion's share—more than two-thirds—of the total quota. The remaining third was divided up among all the other nations given quotas.

The desired effect was obtained. Immigration from the newer sources of Southern and Eastern Europe was reduced to a trickle. The quotas allotted to England and Ireland remained largely unused, as was intended. Total quota immigration fell to a half or a third—and sometimes even less—of the annual limit of 154,000. People from such countries as Greece, or Spain, or Latvia were virtually deprived of any opportunity to come here at all, simply because Greeks or Spaniards or Latvians had not come here before 1920 in any substantial numbers.

The idea behind this discriminatory policy was, to put it baldly, that Americans with English or Irish names were better people and better citizens than Americans with Italian or Greek or Polish names. It was thought that people of West European origin made better citizens than Rumanians or Yugoslavs or Ukrainians or Hungarians or Balts or Austrians. Such a concept is utterly unworthy of our traditions and our ideals. It violates the great political doctrine of the Declaration of Independence that "all men are created equal." It denies the humanitarian creed inscribed beneath the Statue of Liberty proclaiming to all nations, "Give me your tired, your poor, your huddled masses yearning to breathe free." It repudiates our basic religious concepts, our belief in the brotherhood of man, and in the words of St. Paul that "there is neither Jew nor Greek, there is neither bond nor free . . . for ye are all one in Christ Jesus."

The basis of this quota system was false and unworthy in 1924. It is even worse now. At the present time, this quota system keeps out the very people we want to bring in. It is incredible to me that, in this year of 1952, we should again be enacting into law such a slur on the patriotism, the capacity, and the decency of a large part of our citizenry.

Today, we have entered into an alliance, the North Atlantic Treaty, with Italy, Greece, and Turkey against one of the most terrible threats mankind has ever faced [communism]. We are asking them to join with us in protecting the peace of the world. We are helping them to build their defenses, and train their men, in the common cause. But, through this bill we say to their people: You are less worthy to come to this country than Englishmen or Irishmen; you Italians, who need to find homes abroad in the hundreds of thousands—you shall have a quota of 5,645; you Greeks, struggling to assist the helpless victims of a communist civil war—you shall have a quota of 308; and you Turks, you are brave defenders of the Eastern flank, but you shall have a quota of only 225!

Today, we are "protecting" ourselves, as we were in 1924, against being flooded by immigrants from Eastern Europe. This is fantastic. The countries of Eastern Europe have fallen under the communist yoke—they are silenced, fenced off by barbed wire and minefields—no one passes their borders but at the risk of his life. We do not need to be protected against immigrants from these countries—on the contrary we want to stretch out a helping hand, to save those who have managed to flee into Western Europe, to succor those who are brave enough to escape from barbarism, to welcome and restore them against the day when their countries will, as we hope, be free again. But this we cannot do, as we would like to do, because the quota for Poland is only 6,500, as against the 138,000 exiled Poles, all over Europe, who are asking to come to these shores; because the quota for the now subjugated Baltic countries is little more than 700—against the 23,000 Baltic refugees imploring us to admit them to a new life here; because the quota for Rumania is only 289, and some 30,000 Rumanians, who have managed to escape the labor camps and the mass deportations of their Soviet masters, have asked our help. These are only a few examples of the absurdity, the cruelty of carrying over into this year of 1952 the isolationist limitations of our 1924 law.

In no other realm of our national life are we so hampered and stultified by the dead hand of the past, as we are in this field of immigration. We do not limit our cities to their 1920 boundaries—we do not hold our corporations to their 1920 capitalizations—we welcome progress and change to meet changing conditions in every sphere of life, except in the field of immigration.

Finding Better Solutions to the Immigration Problem

The time to shake off this dead weight of past mistakes is now. The time to develop a decent policy of immigration— a fitting instrument for our foreign policy and a true reflection of the ideals we stand for, at home and abroad—is now. . . . I [have] tried to explain to the Congress that the situation we face in immigration is an emergency—that it must be met promptly. I have pointed out that in the last few years, we have blazed a new trail in immigration, through our Displaced Persons Program. Through the combined efforts of the Government and private agencies, working together not to keep people out, but to bring qualified people in, we summoned our resources of good will and human feeling to meet the task. In this program, we have found better techniques to meet the immigration problems of the 1950's.

None of this fruitful experience of the last three years is reflected in this bill before me. None of the crying human needs of this time of trouble is recognized in this bill. But it is not too late. The Congress can remedy these defects, and it can adopt legislation to meet the most critical problems before adjournment.

The only consequential change in the 1924 quota system which the bill would make is to extend a small quota to each of the countries of Asia. But most of the beneficial effects of this gesture are offset by other provisions of the bill. The countries of Asia are told in one breath that they shall have quotas for their nationals, and in the next, that the nationals of the other countries, if their ancestry is as much as 50 percent Asian, shall be charged to these quotas.

It is only with respect to persons of oriental ancestry that this invidious discrimination applies. All other persons are charged to the country of their birth. But persons with Asian ancestry are charged to the countries of Asia, wherever they may have been born, or however long their ancestors have made their homes outside the land of their origin. These provisions are without justification. . . .

We Must Examine Our Immigration Policy

The bill raises basic questions as to our fundamental immigration and naturalization policy, and the laws and practices for putting that policy into effect.

Many of the aspects of the bill which have been most widely criticized in the public debate are reaffirmations or elaborations of existing statutes or administrative procedures. Time and again, examination discloses that the revisions of existing law that would be made by the bill are intended to solidify some restrictive practice of our immigration authorities, or to overrule or modify some ameliorative decision of the Supreme Court or other Federal courts. By and large, the changes that would be made by the bill do not depart from the basically restrictive spirit of our existing laws—but intensify and reinforce it.

These conclusions point to an underlying condition which deserves the most careful study. Should we not undertake a reassessment of our immigration policies and practices in the light of the conditions that face us in the second half of the twentieth century? The great popular interest which this bill has created, and the criticism which it has stirred up, demand an affirmative answer. I hope the Congress will agree to a careful reexamination of this entire matter.

To assist in this complex task, I suggest the creation of a representative commission of outstanding Americans to examine the basic assumptions of our immigration policy, the quota system and all that goes with it, the effect of our present immigration and nationality laws, their administration, and the ways in which they can be brought in line with our national ideals and our foreign policy.

Such a commission should, I believe, be established by the Congress. Its membership should be bi-partisan and divided equally among persons from private life and persons from public life. I suggest that four members be appointed by the President, four by the President of the Senate, and four by the Speaker of the House of Representatives. The commission should be given sufficient funds to employ a staff and it should have adequate powers to hold hearings, take testimony, and obtain information. It should make a report to the President and to the Congress within a year from the time of its creation.

Two Steps Congress Should Take

Pending the completion of studies by such a commission, and the consideration of its recommendations by the Congress, there are certain steps which I believe it is most important for the Congress to take this year.

First, I urge the Congress to enact legislation removing racial barriers against Asians from our laws. Failure to take this step profits us nothing and can only have serious consequences for our relations with the peoples of the far East. A major contribution to this end would be the prompt enactment by the Senate of H.R. 403. That bill, already passed by the House of Representatives, would remove the racial bars to the naturalization of Asians.

Second, I strongly urge the Congress to enact the temporary, emergency immigration legislation which I recommended three months ago. In my message of March 24, 1952, I advised the Congress that one of the gravest problems arising from the present world crisis is created by the overpopulation in parts of Western Europe. That condition is aggravated by the flight and expulsion of people from behind the iron curtain. In view of these serious problems, I asked the Congress to authorize the admission of 300,000 additional immigrants to the United States over a three year period. These immigrants would include Greek nationals, Dutch nationals, Italians from Italy and Trieste, Germans and persons of German ethnic origin, and religious and political refugees from communism in Eastern Europe. This temporary program is urgently needed. It is very important that the Congress act upon it this year. I urge the Congress to give prompt and favorable consideration to the bills introduced by Senator [Robert] Hendrickson and Representative [Emanuel] Celler (S. 3109 and H.R. 7376), which will implement the recommendations contained in my message of March 24.

I very much hope that the Congress will take early action on these recommendations. Legislation to carry them out will correct some of the unjust provisions of our laws, will strengthen us at home and abroad, and will serve to relieve a great deal of the suffering and tension existing in the world today.

The United States Must Reform Its Quota System

ALAN REYNOLDS

The last major change to America's quota system occurred with the passage of the Immigration Act of 1990, which increased the worldwide quota established in 1965 to 700,000. Most of the immigrants who enter under this quota are the family members of U.S. citizens. In the following selection, originally a statement before the House of Representatives on April 21, 1998, Alan Reynolds asserts that family sponsorship unfairly favors immigrants from Asia and Latin America. He contends that United States needs to use different criteria to determine who should be allowed entry into the United States. He recommends an immigration policy modeled on the systems used by Canada and New Zealand, which prioritize immigrants based on their employability and financial assets. Reynolds also suggests controlling immigration by requiring potential immigrants to pay a fee. Reynolds is a senior fellow at the Cato Institute, a libertarian public policy research foundation. He was the director of economic research at the Hudson Institute, a policy research organization that focuses on global security and freedom.

[In 1997] the Hudson Institute published *Workforce 2020*, the sequel to *Workforce 2000*. I did the background research on immigration for this project, and contributed

Alan Reynolds, prepared statement before the U.S. House Subcommittee on Immigration and Claims, Committee on the Judiciary, Washington, DC, April 21, 1998.

some sections of the report. Unlike *Workforce 2000* (which was commissioned by the Department of Labor), *Workforce 2020* was privately funded. My own research has been entirely privately funded. The views I express here are my own, not those of my employer or associates.

Let me begin by quoting a representative passage from the new Hudson study:

> In the 1990s, immigration accounted for fully half of the increase in the labor force; if immigration policy remains unchanged, immigrants will constitute an increasing share of workers in the early twenty-first century. Thus the job qualifications of immigrants will have an increasingly important impact on the skill and education levels of the workforce. Unless they acquire more schooling in the U.S. than they did in their native countries, recent immigrants will account for a rising share of the otherwise dwindling number of Americans who lack a high school education.

Immigration is not inherently good or bad. Given the slowing and aging of the population, a plausible argument could be made that the U.S. might benefit from more rapid increases in the number of working-age immigrants than we have experienced in recent years. There would be more people paying Social Security taxes, for example.

Immigration and the U.S. Labor Force

In my view, the most important immigration issue is not whether the numbers of immigrants should be larger or smaller, but whether or not U.S. policy can prudently continue to be indifferent about inviting huge numbers of permanent residents who lack basic education or language skills.

A few preliminary observations:

1. Growth of the U.S. labor force has already slowed dramatically (from more than 1.6% a year in the 1980s to about 1.1% in the 1990s) and is apt to slow further if tax and transfer policies are not redesigned to improve work incen-

tives for older Americans and second earners. We are running short of willing and able workers. This is likely to be a chronic problem for the foreseeable future. Slow growth of the labor force explains why estimates of future economic growth are closer to 2% than to the 3% norm of the postwar era.

2. Immigration accounted for half of all new additions to the labor force in the first half of this decade. At the margin, when it comes time to add more workers, or to replace retiring workers with young people, immigrations will be increasingly important. The average skill level of U.S. workers, productivity and real wages, may be diluted in the future if too many immigrants bring below-average skills to the job, and are ill-prepared to improve those skills to keep up with the economy's rapid changes.

3. Census assumptions that the sum of legal and illegal immigration can forever be held below 900,000 a year seem unrealistic. External pressures on the borders are not getting any lighter. The population of Asia alone is expected to grow by one billion people by the year 2020, and the population of Latin America and the Caribbean by 155 million.

4. An increased supply of unskilled immigrant workers must depress real wages for unskilled natives unless that increased supply of unskilled labor was matched by increased investment in businesses that make use of unskilled workers. Shifting scarce capital toward low-wage industries is quite unlikely to happen, and it would be wasteful if it did.

5. Concerns about a "shortage" of high-tech employees are misleading. If certain skills become very scarce relative to demand, then salary offers for those jobs will increase— enticing more people to acquire these skills. A better way of putting the issue is that if immigration policy shifted toward putting greater emphasis on immigrants' skills, then skill-based wage differentials would narrow—unskilled jobs would then pay more, and skilled work a bit less. Under current policy, the opposite outcome is more likely, and more troublesome.

6. Under current law, the schooling or skill of legal immigrants is almost 90% a matter of random luck. Two-thirds of immigrants are admitted solely because they have family members living in the United States, and another 16% are refugees or asylees, and 5–6% win the "diversity" lottery. Employment-related criteria have accounted for no more than 13% of immigrants lately, and that figure overstates the true significance of employability due to double counting. Employment-related visas are limited to 140,000, but have been smaller. Work-related visas are often temporary, while the much larger numbers of immigrants admitted regardless of employability are permanent.

De Facto Immigration Quotas

From 1924 to 1965, immigration was rationed according to country of origin. In practice, current policy still does that. This is because the previous wave of immigrants has extremely preferential treatment when it comes to bringing in more relatives from the same countries. The more immigrants who arrived from a certain country in the recent past, the more can be expected from that country in the near future.

From 1990 to 1995, new immigration (aside from legalization under amnesty) averaged about 737,000 a year. Of those, immediate relatives accounted for 238,242 immigrants a year, and family-sponsored relatives accounted for another 220,103. That is, nearly two-thirds (62.2%) of immigrants were admitted solely because they had family members here. This percentage of immigrants in family-sponsored categories has been rising lately—to 63.9% in 1995 and 65.1% in 1996. Another 16% of immigrants in the first half of the nineties (119,000 a year) were refugees and asylees—mainly from former communist countries: the Soviet Union and Eastern Europe, Vietnam, Laos and Cuba.

We have inadvertently restored the old system of favoring immigrants depending on country of origin. But the new favoritism is no longer for immigrants from democratic countries with high levels of prosperity and skill, but for immigrants from the same countries that accounted for the last group of immigrants. This means de facto immigration quotas are heavily biased in favor of aspiring immigrants from Mexico, the former Soviet Union, the Philippines, Vietnam, the Dominican Republic, El Salvador, China, India and Cuba. Recent immigrants from these countries bring in their relatives. And their newly arrived relatives, in turn, sponsor still more relatives from the same countries.

To patch this problem, Congress added "diversity" quotas. The rationing dilemma in this case is so extreme that a lottery is used, with odds not much better than other lotteries. In one 30-day period (ending March 12, 1996), some 6.5 million applications were reportedly received for these 55,000 diversity visas.

With family sponsorship, diversity and refugees using up at least 85% of the available spaces, that does not leave much room for any other criteria, such as employment prospects or investment. The 1990 law permits up to 140,000 employment-based immigrants a year, but the actual figures were only 85,336 in 1995 and 117,499 in 1996. Highly restrictive investment-based criteria (called "employment creation") have admitted only about 500 people each year.

The dominant criteria for U.S. immigration quotas—having a relative here, coming from a really terrible country, or winning the diversity lottery—are obviously unrelated to any concept of what is good for the U.S. economy or society. Instead, the prevailing criteria are limited to just two (among many) conceivable interests of the immigrants themselves namely, escaping from a politically repressive country, or being able to live closer to other family members. Unless Congress is willing to increase the numbers of legal immigrants, any decision to put greater emphasis on employment qualifications requires putting less emphasis on family ties and/or refugee status. If the numbers are limited, there is no choice but to make choices.

Policies in Canada and New Zealand

The percentage of foreign-born residents in Canada is twice as high as it is in the U.S. Yet Canada puts a much higher priority on economic criteria (employability and assets) than the U.S. does, and is also contemplating adding a very strict language requirement. Only half of Canada's immigrants fall into the family reunification category that so dominates U.S. policy, and Canada appears somewhat more strict about refugee qualifications.

Canadian immigrants need 70 out of 100 points. As many as 15 points can be awarded for knowledge of English or French, with another 15 points possible for specific vocational preparation. Education earns up to 12 points. Experience counts for 8 points if the applicant has a job in Canada, which is itself worth another 10–20 points depending on the occupation. Personal suitability and other miscellany make up the balance. An immigration who arrives with a half a million Canadian dollars is rightly considered unlikely to end up dependent on welfare, for example, regardless how those assets are invested. There are also immigration categories for entrepreneurs, the self-employed and investors. Canada also makes limited use of the price system to help balance supply and demand. There is a fee of C$975 for every successful immigrant, with loans available for those unable to pay.

Critics see Canadian policy as harsh, or as a futile exercise in picking winners. But it does at least offer potential immigrants some rules that are not entirely capricious, it does not rely so heavily as the U.S. system on long waiting lists, and it puts a reasonably high priority on the applicant's ability to be financially self-sufficient.

New Zealand actively recruits immigrants, but not without some rules. Applicants must meet "a minimum standard of English" (equivalent to an 11 year old native). Their immigration department notes that "a job offer that is waiting for you is a good way to determine if you are the type of person New Zealand needs." Arriving with "settlement funds" of more than 100,000 New Zealand dollars helps too. The country's point system favors youth, subtracting points after age 30 and noting frankly that "a person over the age of 55 on the Skills category and 64 for the Business Category will not be accepted."

Obviously, the U.S. public might favor quite different standards and priorities than either Canada or New Zealand, if the issue was ever put to them in this way. But so long as immigration depends as heavily as it has on having relatives in the U.S., on being willing to wait a long time, on winning a lottery, or on being granted refugee or asylee status, the U.S. cannot really be said to have any coherent immigration standards at all.

Using Fees to Ration Immigration

Immigration policy is about rationing something of great value—the right to live in the United States. The question boils down to methods and criteria of rationing a relatively small number of spaces among a much larger number of people who would like to live in the United States.

There are only four possible rationing methods—the queue, the lottery, allocation by political or bureaucratic preference, or the price system (a fifth option, of course, is to immigrate illegally). Current policy mainly relies on a mixture of political preference categories and the queue, although the lottery is used too.

Foreigners offered a U.S. job requiring less than two years' experience find themselves in "Employment Third Preference" class, and must wait 10 years for a visa. Permanent residents sponsoring an unmarried child over age 21 are in a family category 2B, which has a 6 year wait. Brothers and sisters of U.S. citizens are in "Family Fourth Preference," which recently had a waiting list of more than one million. Marrying a U.S. citizen can push you ahead in the line, which has created a booming market in mail order brides. Ordinary citizens have no idea how these quotas on importing various categories of people are established, which makes the process vulnerable to the tug and pull of interest groups and log-rolling.

I propose making somewhat more use of the price system, as Canada does, by requiring a modest immigration fee. This would be far more "fair" than relying entirely on arbitrary quotas and multi-year waiting lists. A user fee on immigration services of, say, one or two thousand dollars per accepted immigrant would serve as a means of reducing waiting lists by weeding out marginal applicants with a weak commitment to the U.S. As another example of the price system, a trial program could begin with an auction of diversity quotas, to replace the current use of gambling.

Even with some use of price system, there will still be quotas and queues. The normal problem of the future will not be job creation but the opposite—finding enough qualified workers, to do the work demanded of a high-tech economy. Still, it might be socially soothing to adjust annual immigration quotas downward in recessions, and upward when jobs are plentiful, by adopting a formula that would link a portion of the coming year's immigration quota to unemployment rates in the preceding third quarter.

Sanctioning Illegal Immigration

Half of the problem of illegal immigration is not due to sneaking across the border, but to overstaying legal visas. I propose a system of fines that grows geometrically larger the longer a visa was overdue (e.g., doubled every month). Anyone would be free to leave without paying the fine, or could be deported, but such a person would never again be readmitted without paying the fine plus penalties for late payment. Illegal acts must carry some sanctions for those who commit them, and financial sanctions seem more appropriate. Imprisoning illegal aliens puts their burden on U.S. taxpayers, and wastes limited court time and prison space that could be better devoted to violent criminals.

Those seeking asylum should ask before arriving, like refugees, not just settle here illegally and hire a lawyer. Out of half a million asylee cases received from 1990–94, only 4.5% were approved. This post-1980 opportunity for illegal aliens to remain in the U.S. by going through the motions of applying for asylee status (and often remaining long after the case is denied), is an unnecessary invitation to abuse.

Regardless how many immigrants are legally admitted, a key question is how best to ration valuable immigration rights. What is needed is not another rousing defense of immigration in general, nor an equally indiscriminate closing of the borders, but a serious, comprehensive reexamination of the criteria and methods by which rights to U.S. residence have been regulated.

We must rely on some criteria for determining an immigrant's eligibility. I suggest that the most sensible (and ultimately the most humane) criteria are those that demonstrate the potential immigrant's ability to support himself and his family: formal education, occupational experience, training or other skills (including English language skills), and accumulated savings.

A constructive and compassionate immigration policy must put the primary emphasis on making sure that new entrants have sufficient human and/or financial capital to become productive members of the economy and society.

THE
HISTORY
OF
ISSUES

CHAPTER 4

Confronting Illegal Immigration

Chapter Preface

U ntil the mid-1950s, only a few thousand Cubans immigrated to the United States each year. The Fidel Castro–
led revolution at the end of the decade, which established
a Communist government in Cuba, forever changed relationships between Cuba and the United States. Thousands
of Cubans, fearful of living under the new government, fled
to America which lay a mere ninety miles away. Like many
of the people who enter America, these immigrants were
largely illegal. Unlike most illegal immigrants, however,
those from Cuba enjoyed special privileges for thirty-five
years. The treatment of these Cubans helps show how U.S.
treatment of illegal immigrants varies considerably depending on the immigrants' sending countries.

Coming as it did during the height of the Cold War, the
creation of a Soviet-supported, Communist government in
Cuba prompted the United States to welcome Cubans who
wished to live in a democracy. Cubans who successfully
made the journey to Florida were allowed to remain in the
United States. In stark comparison to most illegal immigrants, these escapees were viewed as having fled political
persecution and thus treated as refugees under the 1952
Walter-McCarran Act. Other immigration laws were passed
specifically to benefit Cubans, notably the Cuban Adjust-
ment Act. Passed in 1966, the law allowed any Cuban who
arrives in the United States illegally to become eligible for
legal status one year and a day after arrival.

The treatment of Cuban immigrants remained constant
until 1994, when a political crisis prompted the Clinton administration to set restrictions on illegal immigration. The
Cuban government blamed deadly riots in Havana on U.S.
foreign policy and announced that it would not prevent

boats from leaving Cuba as long as the United States encouraged illegal immigration. Tens of thousands of Cubans fled, but instead of being welcomed to the United States, they were intercepted and detained. The detentions lasted for eight months, after which the United States and Cuba reached an agreement. In exchange for receiving an additional twenty thousand U.S. immigration slots, Cubans would no longer be automatically granted political refugee status.

The change in policy did not eradicate illegal immigration from Cuba, however, and many immigration analysts charge that Cubans still receive preferential treatment from the United States while Castro remains in power. For example, the "wet feet–dry feet" policy permits Cubans to stay in the United States if they step on shore, although they are returned to Cuba if captured at sea. In contrast, illegal immigrants from Haiti are not afforded such considerations, an inconsistent policy that many people question. As David Simcox, the chairman of the Center for Immigration Studies, writes in *The Caribbean Immigration Centrifuge*, "Washington's policies toward both Cuba and Haiti betray its tendency to see only the short-term political and economic factors in the outflow of Caribbean peoples, ignoring the long-term social and demographic forces driving mass migration from the Caribbean's 22 island nations, whether rich or poor, democratic or dictatorial."

U.S. immigration policy has been modified many times over the past half-century, affecting not only Cubans but also other illegal immigrants, such as those from Mexico. In the following chapter the authors consider how the United States should respond to illegal immigration.

The Creation of Operation Wetback

HANDBOOK OF TEXAS ONLINE

Illegal immigration by Mexicans into the United States has been an issue since the 1920s; the Border Patrol was established in 1924 to control illegal immigration across the U.S.-Mexico border. However, economic considerations caused the U.S. government to loosen its stance on Mexican immigration two decades later. Labor shortages during World War II prompted the United States to look for new sources of workers. In 1942, working with the Mexican government, the U.S. government established the bracero program. The program, which lasted until 1964, permitted Mexicans who otherwise would have entered the United States illegally to legally cross the border to work. By the early 1950s the program was beset by corruption and controversy. Furthermore, even though several hundred thousand Mexican workers were admitted each year under the program, illegal immigration into the United States continued to be a problem. The federal government created Operation Wetback in 1954 as a response to the high level of Mexicans entering the country illegally.

Operation Wetback is described in the following excerpt from the Handbook of Texas Online. *According to the editors, the bracero program encouraged rather than lessened illegal immigration because the legal workers often received lower wages than they would have had they entered the United States illegally. Illegal immigration was especially widespread in Texas because Mexico did not permit the state to partici-*

Handbook of Texas Online, "Operation Wetback," www.tsha.utexas.edu, December 4, 2002. Copyright © 2002 by the Texas State Historical Association. Reproduced by permission.

*pate in the bracero program. Not surprisingly, Operation Wet-
back began in that state. The operation called for the U.S.
Border Patrol and the military to seize illegal immigrants and
send them back to Mexico. The editors note that the number
of immigrants affected by the operation is unknown but is
likely far less than the Immigration and Naturalization Service has claimed. Many critics of the program at the time argued that it was xenophobic and cruel. The* Handbook of
Texas Online *is a collaboration between the Texas State Historical Association and the General Libraries at the University of Texas at Austin.*

Operation Wetback was a repatriation project of the
United States Immigration and Naturalization Service
[INS] to remove illegal Mexican immigrants ("wetbacks")
from the Southwest. During the first decades of the twentieth century, the majority of migrant workers who crossed
the border illegally did not have adequate protection
against exploitation by American farmers. As a result of the
Good Neighbor Policy, Mexico and the United States began
negotiating an accord to protect the rights of Mexican agricultural workers. Continuing discussions and modifications
of the agreement were so successful that the Congress
chose to formalize the "temporary" program into the
Bracero program, authorized by Public Law 78. In the early
1940s, while the program was being viewed as a success in
both countries, Mexico excluded Texas from the labor-
exchange program on the grounds of widespread violation
of contracts, discrimination against migrant workers, and
such violations of their civil rights as perfunctory arrests
for petty causes. Oblivious to the Mexican charges, some
grower organizations in Texas continued to hire illegal Mexican workers and violate such mandates of PL 78 as the requirement to provide workers transportation costs from
and to Mexico, fair and lawful wages, housing, and health
services. World War II and the postwar period exacerbated
the Mexican exodus to the United States, as the demand

for cheap agricultural laborers increased. Graft and corruption on both sides of the border enriched many Mexican officials as well as unethical "coyote" freelancers in the United States who promised contracts in Texas for the unsuspecting Bracero. Studies conducted over a period of several years indicate that the Bracero program increased the number of illegal aliens in Texas and the rest of the country. Because of the low wages paid to legal, contracted braceros, many of them skipped out on their contracts either to return home or to work elsewhere for better wages as wetbacks.

The Bracero Program Collapses

Increasing grievances from various Mexican officials in the United States and Mexico prompted the Mexican government to rescind the bracero agreement and cease the export of Mexican workers. The United States Immigration Service, under pressure from various agricultural groups, retaliated against Mexico in 1951 by allowing thousands of illegals to cross the border, arresting them, and turning them over to the Texas Employment Commission, which delivered them to work for various grower groups in Texas and elsewhere. Over the long term, this action by the federal government, in violation of immigration laws and the agreement with Mexico, caused new problems for Texas. Between 1944 and 1954, "the decade of the wetback," the number of illegal aliens coming from Mexico increased by 6,000 percent. It is estimated that in 1954 before Operation Wetback got under way, more than a million workers had crossed the Rio Grande illegally. Cheap labor displaced native agricultural workers, and increased violation of labor laws and discrimination encouraged criminality, disease, and illiteracy. According to a study conducted in 1950 by the President's Commission on Migratory Labor in Texas, the Rio Grande valley cotton growers were paying approximately half of the wages paid elsewhere in Texas. In 1953 a McAllen newspaper clamored for justice in view of continuing criminal activities by wetbacks. The resulting Operation Wetback, a national reaction against illegal immigration, began in Texas in mid-July 1954. Headed by the commissioner of Immigration and Naturalization Service, Gen. Joseph May Swing, the United States Border Patrol aided by municipal, county, state, and federal authorities, as well as the military, began a quasimilitary operation of search and seizure of all illegal immigrants. Fanning out from the lower Rio Grande valley, Operation Wetback moved northward.

Illegal aliens were repatriated initially through Presidio because the Mexican city across the border, Ojinaga, had rail connections to the interior of Mexico by which workers could be quickly moved on to Durango. A major concern of the operation was to discourage reentry by moving the workers far into the interior. Others were to be sent through El Paso. On July 15, the first day of the operation, 4,800 aliens were apprehended. Thereafter the daily totals dwindled to an average of about 1,100 a day. The forces used by the government were actually relatively small, perhaps no more than 700 men, but were exaggerated by border patrol officials who hoped to scare illegal workers into flight back to Mexico. Valley newspapers also exaggerated the size of the government forces for their own purposes: generally unfavorable editorials attacked the Border Patrol as an invading army seeking to deprive Valley farmers of their inexpensive labor force. While the numbers of deportees remained relatively high, the illegals were transported across the border on trucks and buses. As the pace of the operation slowed, deportation by sea began on the *Emancipation*, which ferried wetbacks from Port Isabel, Texas, to Veracruz, and on other ships. Ships were a preferred mode of transport because they carried the illegal workers farther away from the border than did buses, trucks, or trains. The boat lift continued until the drowning of seven deportees who jumped ship from the *Mercurio* provoked a mutiny and led to a public outcry against the practice in

Mexico. Other aliens, particularly those apprehended in the Midwest states, were flown to Brownsville and sent into Mexico from there. The operation trailed off in the fall of 1954 as INS funding began to run out.

The Scope of the Operation

It is difficult to estimate the number of illegal aliens forced to leave by the operation. The INS claimed as many as 1,300,000, though the number officially apprehended did not come anywhere near this total. The INS estimate rested on the claim that most aliens, fearing apprehension by the government, had voluntarily repatriated themselves before and during the operation. The San Antonio district, which included all of Texas outside of El Paso and the Trans-Pecos, had officially apprehended slightly more than 80,000 aliens, and local INS officials claimed that an additional 500,000 to 700,000 had fled to Mexico before the campaign began. Many commentators have considered these figures to be exaggerated. Various groups opposed any form of temporary labor in the United States. The American G.I. Forum, for instance, by and large had little or no sympathy for the man who crossed the border illegally. Apparently the Texas State Federation of Labor supported the G.I. Forum's position. Eventually the two organizations coproduced a study entitled *What Price Wetbacks?*, which concluded that illegal aliens in United States agriculture damaged the health of the American people, that illegals displaced American workers, that they harmed the retailers of McAllen, and that the open-border policy of the American government posed a threat to the security of the United States. Critics of Operation Wetback considered it xenophobic and heartless.

1996 Laws Concerning Illegal Immigration Are Too Punitive

WILLIAM G. PAUL

Laws targeting illegal immigrants are too harsh, William G. Paul charges in the following selection. Paul criticizes two laws passed by Congress in 1996, the Illegal Immigration Reform and Immigrant Responsibility Act (IIRAIRA) and the Anti-Terrorism and Effective Death Penalty Act. According to Paul, these laws are unfair because they allow for the deportation of immigrants who committed minor crimes, including crimes that occurred before the laws were enacted. He also vilifies the law because illegal immigrants under Immigration and Naturalization Service (INS) custody are denied basic legal rights such as access to an attorney and the right to appeal. Paul charges that these laws ruin the lives of immigrants and tear families apart. He concludes that reforms are necessary to ensure that detentions and deportations are just. Paul is the president of the American Bar Association.

Thousands of immigrants to the U.S. are trapped in the confusing and all-powerful legal net of recently enacted harsh laws, which the Immigration and Naturalization Service (INS) is required to administer. These Federal statutes do not comport with due process standards or the fundamental fairness inherent in the American justice system that protect our citizens. Clearly, there is a double standard for immigrants.

Unfair Standards for Deportation

For example, about the time the controversy over Elian Gonzalez—the six-year-old boy plucked from the coastal waters off Florida after an escape attempt from Cuba took the lives of his mother and several others—first reached fever pitch, a young Chinese girl, captured while trying to enter the U.S. after she fled her homeland, appeared at a review hearing. She was unable to understand English and terribly frightened, and, as tears rolled uncontrollably down her cheeks, she could not wipe them away because her arms were chained to her waist. She must have been in terror, having fled oppression only to be jailed and hauled in chains before strangers, where she understood nothing. She faces deportation.

Moreover, consider the compelling stories of two mothers also subject to deportation. The first is a young German woman who was adopted and brought to Georgia. Now the mother of two, she recently applied for citizenship. Instead, she was ordered deported because, as a teenager, she had entered a guilty plea to charges stemming from pulling the hair of another girl over the affections of a boy.

The second, a young mother in Falls Church, Va., faces deportation and separation from her children because she called the police after being brutally beaten by her husband. Instead of coming to her defense, police arrested her because she bit her husband as he sat on her and repeatedly hit her. Incredibly, both mothers face deportation, while their children—all born here—can remain.

How can a hair-pulling or biting incident be grounds for deportation? Equally important, how has the U.S. become a country that tears apart families or denies due process to those trying to obtain freedom, safety, and prosperity for themselves and their families?

Retroactive Offenses

Answers to both questions are in the Illegal Immigration Reform and Immigrant Responsibility Act (IIRAIRA) and the Anti-Terrorism and Effective Death Penalty Act. Adopted in 1996, these tough laws are at the crux of the problem. They have changed the legal rules for newcomers, making them subject to harsher penalties for infractions than are citizens.

These laws reclassify past infractions retroactively so that they become deportable offenses, even in cases when no prison time was ordered or where there is evidence of rehabilitation. They have widely expanded the definition of aggravated felony to include minor crimes. Noncitizens convicted of aggravated felonies are now not only deportable, but ineligible for a waiver from deportation or for judicial review.

IIRAIRA undermines one of the principles underlying the Constitution—the separation of powers—by removing the historic role of the courts as protectors of individuals from government overreaching. Harsh laws permit those administering them to take harsh action. The INS and its individual agents are authorized by law to detain and deport anyone attempting to enter the U.S. if there is suspicion of fraud, and there is no appeal from these decisions.

The laws have permitted the summary return of victims of torture and persecution to their persecutors, and vested INS agents with the power to banish for 10 years legitimate travelers entering the U.S. on the basis of unsubstantiated allegations of misrepresentation. IIRAIRA also requires imprisoning thousands at great expense to taxpayers. Largely due to this law, the INS has the fastest-growing prisoner populations in the nation. In 1994, it held about 5,500 people. [As of 2000], 17,400 individuals are being held by the INS, which warehouses immigrants in state and local facilities because of the overflow. The INS estimates that, by [the end of 2000], it could be detaining upwards of 23,000 individuals. INS Commissioner Doris Meissner has testified before Congress that the agency is housing more immigrant detainees than its budget will support. She has openly questioned whether the INS should be in the large-scale prison business.

The Treatment of Detainees

The American Bar Association, alarmed about the far-reaching impact of immigration reform and lack of due process for those in INS custody, has held a series of meetings with representatives of the White House, the Justice Department, and the INS. They have resulted in the promulgation of standards for those being held in INS facilities. The standards guarantee access to lawyers, telephones, legal rights presentations, and a limited legal library. However, the INS is unwilling to extend these same standards to local and state facilities, where 60% of all detainees are being held. Shortly, it is expected to issue watered-down and woefully inadequate separate standards for non-INS facilities,[1] which will deny those detained there very fundamental rights, such as access to an attorney.

Detainees often are held in facilities far from their families, support groups, and lawyers, if they are fortunate enough to have legal representation. There have been cases of detainees being transferred from one facility to another without their paperwork, arriving without their jailers knowing the reason for their incarceration. Detainees have been transferred without such personal belongings as their address books, money, and eyeglasses.

The INS routinely refuses to notify a detainee's attorney about his or her transfer. In one case, a lawyer, who had been representing an individual for years, only learned that her client had been moved 1,000 miles and three states away when she went for a routine visit and could not find him. Immigrant advocates maintain that their clients frequently are moved without their advocate being notified.

---

1. The INS issued new detention standards in January 2001 that all facilities, including non-INS facilities, were expected to meet.

These immigration reform laws have created such havoc in the lives of thousands of families that they demand examination.

Unlike Elian Gonzalez, who received special treatment, children and their parents arriving legitimately at ports of entry can encounter one of the most harsh mechanisms put in place by the 1996 law—expedited removal. This gives a low-level government official the right to deport anyone based on mere suspicion of attempted illegal entry, with no appeal. How does this work? After waiting in long lines, international passengers have their passports examined by a uniformed INS agent, who enters their information into a computer and then makes a cursory comparison of the passport picture to the traveler before waving him or her through. Those agents have the power to deport people summarily and ban them from reentering the country for up to 10 years if an INS agent believes the documents "don't look right" or if there is something "suspicious" about a traveler.

A Violation of American Principles

Additionally, those fleeing oppression and arriving in the U.S. without any papers at all are arrested, imprisoned, and may ultimately be sent back to the country they fled. Moreover, once the decision has been made, there is no appeal—even when the agent is proven wrong. Expedited removal violates the very fundamentals of our nation's principles of justice, fairness, and decency by giving INS agents full authority to be prosecutor, judge, and jury, and stripping away the right to due process.

Take the case of Sonia, who arrived at Miami International Airport from Venezuela shortly after the new immigration laws were enacted. She expected to use her visitor's visa to visit her children, who are students, as she had done in the past. Instead, Sonia was detained for 36 hours, humiliated, mistreated, subjected to strip searches, fed nothing, and then forced to sign papers that banned her from entering the country for five years—all without legal representation. "This was the most shameful and humiliating day that I have ever had," she recalled. "That horrible, dark, and gloomy day came with no mercy at all."

As part of the expedited removal process, Sonia was held without counsel for three days and denied access to a telephone. She was deported despite having a valid visa issued by the U.S. Embassy in Caracas. Finally worn out and worn down, Sonia signed documents admitting that she had attempted to enter the U.S. fraudulently, even though her papers were valid.

Sonia does not blame the U.S. "I know what a totalitarian regime is—where the people are only trash and where they have no rights to anything," she said. "I know that [America] is not a country like this."

Individuals can be imprisoned for life if the U.S. has no relations with the country they left. These "lifers" become stuck in jail limbo, as were the Cubans who took hostages in 1999 in Louisiana after spending more than a dozen years in captivity. In an isolated act, the U.S. negotiated a highly unusual agreement during the zenith of the Elian Gonzalez frenzy, in which the Cuban government accepted those Cubans back, then imprisoned them upon their return.

While no one condones hostage-taking, harsh laws can prompt harsh reactions. In Florida, outside the Krome Detention Center near Miami, a hunger strike was launched by the desperate and frustrated mothers of Cuban lifers who had been locked away for years, far from family and community support. After several weeks, and with growing public support, the INS responded to the mothers' demands and ordered their sons transferred back to Florida. Five were eventually released. Mandatory detention can trap many in this limbo. It requires that all INS detainees awaiting deportation must be held, making them the only prisoners in the U.S. with no right to an individual bond hearing. Under the American legal system, even people charged with a capital offense have a right to a bond hearing. Applied in conjunction with other immigration reform laws, mandatory detention has tripled the number of individuals being held by the INS.

An Overly Harsh Law

Another provision of IIRAIRA is aggravated felony, which reclassifies past crimes of noncitizens to more serious and deportable offenses, even if they have already served their time for the infractions, have been rehabilitated, or never spent a day in jail.

There have been many cases of people being stopped at U.S. borders as they attempt to enter to conduct business. For some of these individuals, when INS agents check their passports and computerized information, they may find a past infraction—now reclassified retroactively to a more serious offense. These people can no longer enter, or—as in the case of a Canadian businessman found to have passed a few bad checks 20 years earlier—they are jailed.

Rep. Sheila Jackson Lee (D.-Tex.) has questioned the soundness and constitutionality of mandatory detention. She maintains that any individual who has family ties, is not a danger to the community, is not likely to abscond, and has posted bond should be released. Jackson Lee asserts that restoring discretion to the INS on whether to detain or deport individuals would not only ensure fairness, but alleviate the INS burden. She is not alone in reexamining the harsh 1996 legislation. Several bills are pending in Washington to amend portions of the law.

Rep. Bill McCollum (R.-Fla.), once a staunch IIRAIRA supporter, wants another look. "The 1996 law went too far," maintains McCollum, who has introduced remedial legislation. "We are a just and fair nation and must strike a just and fair balance in our immigration laws."

Reps. Barney Frank (D.-Mass.), Martin Frost (D.-Tex.), and Lincoln Diaz-Balart (R.-Fla.) have introduced amendments to provide long-term legal residents a day in court. Among other changes, the proposed amendments would provide a chance to consider an individual's family life, length of residency, community contributions, and military service before requiring deportation.

Ill Treatment of African and Asian Immigrants

When originally considering IIRAIRA, some of its supporters maintained that minor crimes such as shoplifting would not be grounds for deportation. Tell that to Olufolake Olaleye, a Nigerian living in Atlanta. This mother of two was ordered deported because of a conviction on charges of shoplifting baby clothes worth $14.99.

Olaleye entered the U.S. legally in 1984, becoming a permanent resident in 1990. She worked as a gas station cashier and never asked for, or received, public benefits. In 1993, while attempting to return baby outfits without a receipt, Olaleye was accused of shoplifting, given a citation, and told to appear in court. Faced with a problem she considered a misunderstanding, Olaleye appeared without a lawyer.

After explaining the circumstances to the judge, she entered a guilty plea she said was to put a quick end to the matter. She was fined $360 and received a 12-month suspended sentence and 12 months probation, which was terminated two months later when she paid the fine. At the time, there were no negative immigration consequences for Olaleye. She was accepted for citizenship and awaited a swearing-in date. Subsequently, IIRAIRA became law and the INS reopened her file. She was ordered deported as an "aggravated felon."

Or how about the case of the young woman from Sri Lanka, having fled civil war and torture, only to arrive in Chicago and have her child taken away from her? This woman, who speaks no English, was jailed. For weeks, unable to communicate with those around her, she was frantic to learn the fate of her child. Amnesty International caught wind of her case and asked local advocates to investigate.

They did and found the child unharmed in foster care.

"This is a country that respects people's rights. I come here because this country is a freedom country for me to raise my family," Bi Meng Zheng said while in the INS Detention Center in San Pedro, Calif. He fled China for the promise of freedom. Instead, he was jailed after he missed his first immigration court hearing.

Zheng, who never committed a crime, spent four years locked behind bars after he was ordered deported because China refused to accept him back. He was released only after human rights advocates campaigned zealously for his freedom.

Let us hope his life in a free country meets his expectations. More importantly, let us hope his new nation meets its promises of freedom and a better way of life.

This [viewpoint] recounts the stories of just a few caught in a trap after pursuing the dream of freedom. It gives them faces, resonance, and sympathy. What about the lives and the plight of thousands of others being jailed and deported? What does it say about us, that we cannot promise them a fair hearing? The U.S., a nation of immigrants, cannot be free if it takes freedom from those who believe in the promise of justice for all.

IIRAIRA has taken us down the wrong path. We must set out on a new and better course.

The Lesson of Elian Gonzalez: America Must Change Its Treatment of Child Refugees

MARVIN P. DAWKINS

One of the biggest stories in 1999 and 2000 was the saga of Elian Gonzalez, a young Cuban boy who was rescued off the coast of Miami after he and his mother, who died in the attempt, tried to illegally emigrate from Cuba, a nation whose Communist government has long been opposed by the United States. His father, who had remained in Cuba, sought the return of Elian. After nearly five months of debate and a controversial raid on the home where Elian was staying, the boy was sent back to Cuba. His story prompted a larger discussion on America's treatment of all refugees, who often attempt to enter the United States illegally to escape political or economic persecution.

In an April 2000 article, Marvin P. Dawkins argues that the U.S. government must reconsider its treatment of child refugees, particularly those from Haiti, a country that has held democratic elections and has received political and economic support from the United States. He argues that Cuban refugees are treated better than their Haitian counterparts,

Marvin P. Dawkins, "Rethinking U.S. Immigration Policy," *Black Issues in Higher Education,* vol. 17, April 27, 2000. Copyright © 2000 by Cox, Matthews, & Associates. Reproduced by permission.

who are usually sent back to their homeland immediately. Ac-
cording to Dawkins, the United States is morally obligated to
protect all children, regardless of the political relationship
America has with the refugees' home countries. Dawkins is
a professor of sociology at the University of Miami.

F rom the looks of things, it's all about Elian. The immigration saga has offered political intrigue and heart-tugging
soap opera. Almost from the start, U.S. officials, adhering
to current policy, insisted Elian should be returned to his
father in Cuba. His American relatives, meanwhile, dug in
for a long siege, with a unified Cuban community rallying
around their resistance to this ruling. The manner in which
Elian Gonzalez entered the United States and the ensuing
tug-of-war between his relatives in Miami and Cuba have
led many to question the guiding principles behind current
U.S. immigration policy, particularly provisions enacted by
the U.S. Congress to speed up the investigation process,
thereby making it easier for immigration officials to deport
illegal immigrants.

Haiti Versus Cuba

But in truth, it's not all about Elian. Although attention has
been focused on the 6-year-old, this child's case is inextri-
cably linked to the fate of thousands of other children who
have entered the United States from Haiti, Mexico and
other nations under equally extraordinary circumstances.
The difference is, those children were sent back to their
home country by immigration officials following a relatively brief interview operating under current law. But the
protracted case of Elian Gonzalez has stimulated public debate that should be extended to a re-examination of current immigration policy as it affects children.

For decades, the United States has maintained its immigration policy of accepting Cubans who risk their lives on
the sea fleeing Communist-controlled Cuba for Miami. At the
same time, the United States largely rejects Haitians and oth-

ers who attempt to enter the country through similar means. This policy, dating back to the beginnings of the Cold War, has been defended on the grounds that Cubans are "political" refugees, while Haitians are "economic" refugees.

This distinction has been at the heart of the difference in treatment of Haitian and Cuban refugees, with the former usually suffering the consequence of being immediately sent back to their homeland. The treatment of Haitian immigrants has not been changed despite vehement protest by and on behalf of the Haitian community in Miami.

The Fate of Refugee Children

The Elian case raises an important question: What should be at the heart of U.S. immigration policy in considering the fate of all children, including those who arrive from Cuba and Haiti?

The expression that "what is best for the child" has been used repeatedly as the guiding principle by both sides. Notwithstanding the merits of the arguments on both sides of the dispute, applying this principle more generally high-

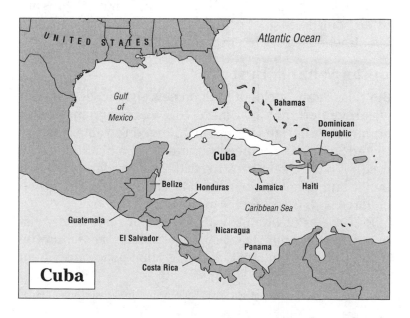

lights the absurdity of the current policy, which ignores what is in the "best interest" of a Haitian child by sending that child back to an almost certain life of despair. Some proposed solutions in the Elian Gonzalez case have rightly called for changing immigration policy to widen the options beyond the narrow alternatives that restrict immigration officials under current law. Clearly, the best thing that could come out of the Elian Gonzalez case would be constructive debate with an eye toward retooling current policy. We need to make America's moral obligation to protect children the central principle in dealing with immigrants, whether from Cuba, Haiti, Mexico or other nations.

The need for "child protection" immigration policy was graphically illustrated in the early days of the Gonzalez case. When little Elian was discovered off the Florida coast, the reaction of people in the United States was to embrace this child.

At about the same time, a separate incident occurred. A boatload of Haitians was intercepted before reaching the United States, and most of those on board were sent back to Haiti. Immigration officials determined that this was another routine case of returning to their home country, people who attempt to enter the United States illegally.

Doing What Is Best

But this routine incident took on new significance when it was revealed that a woman who was pregnant and ill among the Haitians had been allowed to remain in the United States but had been separated from her young children, who were sent back to Haiti. This revelation led to a public outcry and the eventual decision to reunite the two children with their mother in the United States.

Regardless of who prevails in the Gonzalez family dispute,[1] the most significant outcome of Elian's case may be that it shifts the focus of U.S. immigration policy away from

1. In 2000 the U.S. government sent Elian back to Cuba to live with his father.

the principle of "how quickly can we deport people" to "doing what is best for children."

The political relationship between the United States and the home country should not be the primary basis for deciding what is best for children. Hopefully, Elian Gonzalez will be the catalyst for further national debate over immigration, and this debate will lead to the creation of laws that change the treatment of thousands of children.

The U.S.-Canadian Border Must Be Strengthened

WASHINGTON TIMES

The terrorist attacks of September 11, 2001, prompted a re-examination of America's border control efforts and the nation's ability to keep people who might pose a security threat from entering. Much of this debate focuses on the United States–Mexico border, ignoring the 80 million people who cross the border between Canada and the United States each year. In the following editorial, published in December 2003, the Washington Times *asserts that the federal government is ignoring the threat of illegal immigration across the U.S.-Canada border. According to the newspaper, Canadian efforts to secure its border and prevent terrorists from entering North America have proven ineffective, as the entrance of an Algerian terrorist into Canada proves. The* Washington Times *contends that the United States must adequately fund efforts to secure its northern border.*

While the federal government focuses its attention and resources on combating illegal immigration and drug trafficking from Mexico, the United States ignores at its peril the dangers on its 4,121-mile border with Canada. More than 45 million cars and trucks, along with 80 million people, will cross the border this year [2003] from Canada into the United States. Any one of these people or vehicles could be hiding illegal aliens, carrying terrorists, transporting drugs or concealing weapons of mass destruction. These vehicles will be met by an undermanned force of immigration and customs inspectors, and a thinly stretched line of border agents. America must do a better job of securing the U.S.-Canada border.

A two-month investigation by the *Washington Times* of ports of entry from Washington state to Maine found that guarding the northern border had never been a priority for the White House or Capitol Hill, and that the failure to adequately fund security efforts along the northern border had forced the federal government to play catch up following the September 11 [, 2001, terrorist] attacks. Moreover, there is no information, and the U.S. government does not even have an estimate, of the number of illegals who enter this country each year from Canada. What is known is that the numbers are growing and that some of those attempting to sneak in could be terrorists. According to the newly formed Bureau of Customs and Border Protection (BCP), illegal immigrants from as many as 60 countries—including Afghanistan, Pakistan, Algeria, Yemen and Mexico—are apprehended each year attempting to illegally enter the United States from Canada. Al Qaeda and Hezbollah are among the terrorist organizations present there. Both have a history of targeting Americans and may be interested in staging attacks on the United States in the future. Since 1995, at least 15 persons identified by federal authorities as terrorists have been caught attempting to cross the border from Canada into the United States.

An Algerian Terrorist Enters Canada

Canada has taken steps since September 11 to strengthen its own border control efforts. These include new initiatives to identify and prosecute terrorists, to prevent terrorists from entering Canada and to keep the U.S.-Canada border secure. The problem is that approximately 300,000 immigrants are admitted to Canada each year, including some identified as terrorists by law-enforcement authorities.

One such individual was Ahmed Ressam, an Algerian who used a fraudulent French passport to enter Canada in 1994. He requested political asylum from Canadian authorities, claiming to have been tortured in Algeria and falsely accused of terrorist activities. Without checking with the Algerian government, Canadian authorities released Ressam. He moved into an apartment complex in Montreal that was the headquarters of a terrorist cell connected to al Qaeda. In 1998, he traveled to Afghanistan, where he attended an al Qaeda training camp. In December 1999, Ressam was arrested by customs inspectors in Port Angeles, Wash., as he tried to enter the United States. He was subsequently convicted of attempting to bomb Los Angeles International Airport during the millennium celebrations.

The unfortunate reality is that—given the laxity of Canadian border control policies over the years—it is entirely possible, if not likely, that there are more Ressams hidden in Canada, waiting for the opportunity to sneak across the border to kill large numbers of Americans. It is essential that the United States press Canada to take further actions to uproot the terrorists who migrated there by falsely claiming to be refugees. Equally important, the United States must provide adequate resources to enable our own guardians of the border to do their job.

The United States Should Grant Temporary Legal Status to Undocumented Immigrants

GEORGE W. BUSH

Illegal immigration has been at the forefront of America's im-
migration debate since the middle of the twentieth century.
In the following selection, originally a speech given in Janu-
ary 2004, President George W. Bush outlines his plan for a
temporary worker program that would offer legal status to un-
documented immigrants who are already working in the
United States. The president explains that these workers
would fill jobs that American citizens are not willing to take.
They would be allowed to stay in the United States legally for
three years or longer, pending renewal of their status. Accord-
ing to Bush, the temporary workers would be expected to re-
turn to their home countries after their period of work has ex-
pired, and would also be granted financial incentives, such
as being able to put some of their earnings into a savings ac-
count that they could withdraw from when they returned
home. Temporary workers would also be eligible to apply for
U.S. citizenship. The president asserts that his proposal does
not give amnesty to illegal immigrants, but instead is a way

George W. Bush, "President Bush Proposes New Temporary Worker Program,"
www.whitehouse.gov, January 7, 2004.

for previously illegal immigrants to contribute to the United States and possibly become citizens. As of August 2005 Congress had not voted on his proposal. Bush is the forty-third president of the United States.

Many of you here today are Americans by choice, and you have followed in the path of millions. And over the generations we have received energetic, ambitious, optimistic people from every part of the world. By tradition and conviction, our country is a welcoming society. America is a stronger and better nation because of the hard work and the faith and entrepreneurial spirit of immigrants.

Successful Assimilation

Every generation of immigrants has reaffirmed the wisdom of remaining open to the talents and dreams of the world. And every generation of immigrants has reaffirmed our ability to assimilate newcomers—which is one of the defining strengths of our country.

During one great period of immigration—between 1891 and 1920—our nation received some 18 million men, women and children from other nations. The hard work of these immigrants helped make our economy the largest in the world. The children of immigrants put on the uniform and helped to liberate the lands of their ancestors. One of the primary reasons America became a great power in the 20th century is because we welcomed the talent and the character and the patriotism of immigrant families.

The contributions of immigrants to America continue. About 14 percent of our nation's civilian workforce is foreign-born. Most begin their working lives in America by taking hard jobs and clocking long hours in important industries. Many immigrants also start businesses, taking the familiar path from hired labor to ownership.

As a Texan, I have known many immigrant families, mainly from Mexico, and I have seen what they add to our country. They bring to America the values of faith in God, love of family, hard work and self reliance—the values that made us a great nation to begin with. We've all seen those values in action, through the service and sacrifice of more than 35,000 foreign-born men and women currently on active duty in the United States military. One of them is Master Gunnery Sergeant Guadalupe Denogean, an immigrant from Mexico who has served in the Marine Corps for 25 years and counting. [In 2003], I was honored and proud to witness Sergeant Denogean take the oath of citizenship in a hospital where he was recovering from wounds he received in Iraq. I'm honored to be his Commander-in-Chief, I'm proud to call him a fellow American.

Illegal Immigrants Are Exploited

As a nation that values irnmigration, and depends on immigration, we should have immigration laws that work and make us proud. Yet today we do not. Instead, we see many employers turning to the illegal labor market. We see millions of hard-working men and women condemned to fear and insecurity in a massive, undocumented economy. Illegal entry across our borders makes more difficult the urgent task of securing the homeland. The system is not working. Our nation needs an immigration system that serves the American economy, and reflects the American Dream.

Reform must begin by confronting a basic fact of life and economics: some of the jobs being generated in America's growing economy are jobs American citizens are not filling. Yet these jobs represent a tremendous opportunity for workers from abroad who want to work and fulfill their duties as a husband or a wife, a son or a daughter.

Their search for a better life is one of the most basic desires of human beings. Many undocumented workers have walked mile after mile, through the heat of the day and the cold of the night. Some have risked their lives in dangerous desert border crossings, or entrusted their lives to the brutal rings of heartless human smugglers. Workers who seek only to earn a living end up in the shadows of American life—fearful, often abused and exploited. When they are victimized by crime, they are afraid to call the police, or seek recourse in the legal system. They are cut off from their families far away, fearing if they leave our country to visit relatives back home, they might never be able to return to their jobs.

The situation I described is wrong. It is not the American way. Out of common sense and fairness, our laws should allow willing workers to enter our country and fill jobs that Americans are not filling. We must make our immigration laws more rational, and more humane. And I believe we can do so without jeopardizing the livelihoods of American citizens.

Four Basic Principles

Our reforms should be guided by a few basic principles. First, America must control its borders. Following the attacks of September the 11th, 2001, this duty of the federal government has become even more urgent. And we're fulfilling that duty.

For the first time in our history, we have consolidated all border agencies under one roof to make sure they share information and the work is more effective. We're matching all visa applicants against an expanded screening list to identify terrorists and criminals and immigration violators. [In January 2004], we have begun using advanced technology to better record and track aliens who enter our country—and to make sure they leave as scheduled. We have deployed new gamma and x-ray systems to scan cargo and containers and shipments at ports of entry to America. We have significantly expanded the Border Patrol—with more than a thousand new agents on the borders, and 40 percent greater funding [since 2002]. We're working closely with the Canadian and Mexican governments to increase border security. America is acting on a basic belief: our borders should be open to legal travel and honest trade; our borders should be shut and barred tight to criminals, to drug traders, to drug traffickers and to criminals, and to terrorists.

Second, new immigration laws should serve the economic needs of our country. If an American employer is offering a job that American citizens are not willing to take, we ought to welcome into our country a person who will fill that job.

Third, we should not give unfair rewards to illegal immigrants in the citizenship process or disadvantage those who came here lawfully, or hope to do so.

Fourth, new laws should provide incentives for temporary, foreign workers to return permanently to their home countries after their period of work in the United States has expired.

Today, I ask the Congress to join me in passing new immigration laws that reflect these principles, that meet America's economic needs, and live up to our highest ideals.

A New Approach to Immigration

I propose a new temporary worker program that will match willing foreign workers with willing American employers, when no Americans can be found to fill the jobs. This program will offer legal status, as temporary workers, to the millions of undocumented men and women now employed in the United States, and to those in foreign countries who seek to participate in the program and have been offered employment here. This new system should be clear and efficient, so employers are able to find workers quickly and simply.

All who participate in the temporary worker program must have a job, or, if not living in the United States, a job offer. The legal status granted by this program will last three years and will be renewable—but it will have an end. Participants who do not remain employed, who do not follow the rules of the program, or who break the law will not be eligible for continued participation and will be required to return to their home.

Under my proposal, employers have key responsibilities. Employers who extend job offers must first make every reasonable effort to find an American worker for the job at hand. Our government will develop a quick and simple system for employers to search for American workers. Employers must not hire undocumented aliens or temporary workers whose legal status has expired. They must report to the government the temporary workers they hire, and who leave their employ, so that we can keep track of people in the program, and better enforce immigration laws. There must be strong workplace enforcement with tough penalties for anyone, for any employer violating these laws.

Undocumented workers now here will be required to pay a one-time fee to register for the temporary worker program. Those who seek to join the program from abroad, and have complied with our immigration laws, will not have to pay any fee. All participants will be issued a temporary worker card that will allow them to travel back and forth between their home and the United States without fear of being denied re-entry into our country.

This program expects temporary workers to return permanently to their home countries after their period of work in the United States has expired. And there should be financial incentives for them to do so. I will work with foreign governments on a plan to give temporary workers credit, when they enter their own nation's retirement system, for the time they have worked in America. I also support making it easier for temporary workers to contribute a portion of their earnings to tax-preferred savings accounts, money they can collect as they return to their native countries. After all, in many of those countries, a small nest egg is what is necessary to start their own business, or buy some land for their family.

Increasing the Number of Citizens

Some temporary workers will make the decision to pursue American citizenship. Those who make this choice will be allowed to apply in the normal way. They will not be given unfair advantage over people who have followed legal procedures from the start. I oppose amnesty, placing undocumented workers on the automatic path to citizenship. Granting amnesty encourages the violation of our laws, and perpetuates illegal immigration. America is a welcoming country, but citizenship must not be the automatic reward for violating the laws of America.

The citizenship line, however, is too long, and our current limits on legal immigration are too low. My administration will work with the Congress to increase the annual number of green cards that can lead to citizenship. Those willing to take the difficult path of citizenship—the path of work, and patience, and assimilation—should be welcome in America, like generations of immigrants before them.

In the process of immigration reform, we must also set high expectations for what new citizens should know. An understanding of what it means to be an American is not a formality in the naturalization process, it is essential to full participation in our democracy. My administration will examine the standard of knowledge in the current citizenship test. We must ensure that new citizens know not only the facts of our history, but the ideals that have shaped our history. Every citizen of America has an obligation to learn the values that make us one nation: liberty and civic responsibility, equality under God, and tolerance for others.

This new temporary worker program will bring more than economic benefits to America. Our homeland will be more secure when we can better account for those who enter our country, instead of the current situation in which millions of people are unknown, unknown to the law. Law enforcement will face fewer problems with undocumented workers, and will be better able to focus on the true threats to our nation from criminals and terrorists. And when temporary workers can travel legally and freely, there will be more efficient management of our borders and more effective enforcement against those who pose a danger to our country.

A Fair and Compassionate System

This new system will be more compassionate. Decent, hard-working people will now be protected by labor laws, with the right to change jobs, earn fair wages, and enjoy the same working conditions that the law requires for American workers. Temporary workers will be able to establish their identities by obtaining the legal documents we all take for granted. And they will be able to talk openly to authorities, to report crimes when they are harmed, without the fear of being deported.

The best way, in the long run, to reduce the pressures that create illegal immigration in the first place is to expand economic opportunity among the countries in our neighborhood. In a few days I will go to Mexico for the Special Summit of the Americas, where we will discuss ways to advance free trade, and to fight corruption, and encourage the reforms that lead to prosperity. Real growth and real hope in the nations of our hemisphere will lessen the flow of new immigrants to America when more citizens of other countries are able to achieve their dreams at their own home.

Yet our country has always benefited from the dreams that others have brought here. By working hard for a better life, immigrants contribute to the life of our nation. The temporary worker program I am proposing today represents the best tradition of our society, a society that honors the law, and welcomes the newcomer. This plan will help return order and fairness to our immigration system, and in so doing we will honor our values, by showing our respect for those who work hard and share in the ideals of America.

May God bless you all.

Giving Amnesty to Illegal Immigrants Will Destroy America

WILLIAM NORMAN GRIGG

One approach to controlling illegal immigration is through amnesty—giving illegal immigrants temporary legal status that will place them on the path toward becoming legal residents and citizens. In the following selection William Norman Grigg argues that a proposal made by President George W. Bush in 2004 will have a negative impact on the United States. While the president asserts that the proposal, which would allow illegal immigrants to work in the United States temporarily, is not an amnesty program, Grigg argues otherwise. Grigg asserts that granting legal status to millions of illegal immigrants would increase immigration and blur the distinctions between American and Mexican cultures. He also maintains that these immigrants would take away jobs from Americans and drive down wages. Grigg concludes that the Bush administration is making too many concessions to the Mexican government in hopes of improving its relationship with its southern neighbor, a relationship often made tense due to the problem of illegal immigration. Grigg is the senior editor of the magazine New America. *The president's plan had not become law as of August 2005.*

President [George W.] Bush's proposed immigration reform package is a shocking betrayal of our nation's sovereignty, culture and economy. It must not be allowed to pass.[1]

Bill Clinton uttered countless deceptive words during his eight-year occupancy of the White House, but perhaps none captured the essence of his slippery dishonesty better than these: "It depends on what the meaning of the word 'is' is." In defending his proposed amnesty for millions of illegal aliens, George W. Bush is striving to set a new record for brazen presidential dishonesty.

"This plan is not amnesty, placing undocumented workers on the automatic path of citizenship," insisted Mr. Bush at a January 12 [2004] press conference in Monterrey, Mexico, as he stood alongside Mexican President Vicente Fox. "I oppose amnesty because it encourages the violation of our laws and perpetuates illegal immigration."

Rewarding Illegal Immigration

As has often been said, crime unpunished is crime rewarded. In his January 7 White House address calling for a "new temporary worker program," the president outlined a plan that would reward those who violated our immigration laws by jumping the queue and taking up residence here illegally:

• The president proposed "legal status, as temporary workers, to the millions of undocumented men and women now employed in the United States, and to those in foreign countries who seek to participate in the program and have been offered employment here";

• That temporary legal status, the president said, "will last three years and will be renewable";

• Mr. Bush claimed that "our current limits on legal immigration are too low." He added that his administration will work with Congress to "increase the annual number of

1. Congress has not voted on the package as of August 2005.

green cards that can lead to citizenship" for illegal aliens currently residing here, as well as others arriving every day in anticipation of being legalized once the proposal goes into effect.

It's vitally important to recognize that the Bush plan would not be limited to the current illegal alien population, which is commonly estimated to be 6–12 million (but may be 20 million or more). As the president's own words demonstrate, it would also extend to "those in foreign countries who seek to participate in the program."

Supposedly, those coming from foreign countries would need a job offer in advance of their arrival. But the president's invitation had an immediate, and quite predictable, effect. "The U.S. Border Patrol marks January 7 as the day illegal crossing numbers surge," reported a January 10 *Arizona Star* dispatch from the Mexican border town of Hermosillo. "We're starting to see an increase already," commented Border Patrol spokesman Andy Adame. It's reasonable to expect that a similar "amnesty rush" is underway elsewhere as millions—or tens of millions—of others race to take advantage of the Bush plan.

The Border Will Vanish

Ah, but that plan isn't an amnesty, insists the president, clinging to his official fiction with Clintonian tenacity. Representative Ron Paul (R-Texas) has no use for such evasions. "Millions of people who broke the law by entering, staying, and working in our country will not be punished, but rather rewarded with a visa," comments Rep. Paul. "This is amnesty, plain and simple. Lawbreakers are given legal status, while those seeking to immigrate legally face years of paperwork and long waits for a visa."

More disturbing still is the fact that the Bush plan represents merely the first installment. The Mexican regime has already broadcast demands for further concessions. Mexican President Fox offered honeyed words of support for the Bush plan during his January 12 joint press conference with Bush. But prior to Bush's trip to Monterrey, Fox had told the Mexican press that the Bush plan "es más pequeñito de lo que buscamos" ("it's much smaller than what we're looking for"). And Mexico's *El Universal* had reported, "The secretary of Foreign Relations, Luis Ernesto Derbez, affirmed that [Fox] cannot be satisfied with George W. Bush's proposal to grant temporary employment to immigrants. . . . The goal is a total and complete program that protects those [Mexicans] in the United States and those who aspire to go there."

The Mexican regime will be satisfied with nothing less than the abolition of our southern border, and our absorption of as many people as that government sees fit to send north. Eventually, the process begun by the Bush plan would "solve" the illegal immigration problem by simply removing our borders altogether—and by effectively destroying the concept of U.S. citizenship as well.

Creating an Immigration Chain

Supposedly, the newly legalized "temporary workers" would return to their home countries after the permits expire.

"My proposal expects that most temporary workers will eventually return permanently to their home countries when the period of work that I will be negotiating with Congress has expired," explained the president in Monterrey. Toward that end, he continued, "I'll work with [Mexican] President Fox and other leaders on a plan to give temporary workers credit in their home countries' retirement systems for the time they work in the United States."

The administration's proposal would also "reduce the cost of sending money home to families and local communities," continued the president. Such remittances from Mexican workers in America are that nation's second-largest source of foreign income. Additionally, as the president pointed out, through the Inter-American Development Bank "we"—meaning American taxpayers—"are expanding access to credit for small business entrepreneurs" in Mexico and elsewhere in Latin America.

All of this taxpayer-funded largesse is necessary, insists the president, in order to "reduce the pressures that create illegal immigration" by expanding economic opportunity south of our border. But the amnesty itself creates a powerful incentive for newly legalized immigrants to establish themselves here and begin the process of chain immigration, through which untold millions of new immigrants would be brought in. This is what happened with the most recent immigration amnesty in 1986.

In anticipation of George W. Bush's "compassionate conservative" rhetoric, former Senator Alan Simpson of Wyoming, the chief sponsor of the 1986 Immigration Reform and Control Act (IRCA), insisted that the earlier amnesty was "a humane approach to immigration reform." Simpson also admitted at the time, "I don't know what the impact will be." Eighteen years later, we now know the impact: 6–12 million, and possibly 20 million or more, illegal aliens. If amnesty is granted to that population, and it begins the process of chain immigration of relatives from abroad, and it is supplemented by millions of others who come here based on job offers extended through Bush's temporary worker program, we might as well disband the border patrol and discontinue the fiction of having immigration controls at all.

Bad for American Workers

President Bush's concern for the economic plight of illegal aliens in our midst is as puzzling as his indifference to the economic circumstances of American workers.

"Over the past 10 years, more than 2 million low-skilled American workers have been displaced from their jobs," writes CNN financial analyst Lou Dobbs. "And each 10 percent increase in the immigrant workforce decreases U.S. wages by 3.5 percent." Mr. Bush and his political allies blithely assure the public that illegal immigrants are doing jobs nobody wants. However, points out Steve Camarota of the Center for Immigration Studies, "what they really mean is that they are doing jobs that they as middle- and upper-class people don't want."

"Massive immigration is vastly more popular among the elites than among the public," Steve Sailer, president of the Human Biodiversity Institute, told the *New American*. "Lawyers, politicians, and business executives won't find their pay driven down much by increased competition. On the other hand, if I was, say, a carpenter, I'd be horrified by what the President of the United States is planning to do to me and my family. What's the global average wage made by carpenters? I'd be surprised if it were more than 33 percent of the average American carpenter's wage, and I wouldn't be shocked if it were only 10 percent as much."

"It's all a matter of supply and demand," explains Sailer. "As they teach you during the first week of Econ 101, when the supply of labor goes up its price [wage] goes down. . . . The only restriction the Bush people are talking about is that the job offers to foreigners must meet the minimum wage. That's $5.15 per hour, or $10,712 for a full-time worker."

Sailer describes the Bush plan as "a globalist libertarian's fantasy. It's essentially identical to the *Wall Street Journal* editorial page's long campaign for a constitutional amendment reading 'There shall be open borders.'" This would mean not only a deluge of low-skilled, low-paid labor from Mexico, but from across the globe. According to Dobbs, "for all the world the president's [immigration proposal] . . . sounds like a national job fair for those businesses and farms that don't want to pay a living wage and for those foreigners who correctly think U.S. border security is a joke and are willing to break our laws to live here."

The immediate beneficiaries would be illegal workers from Mexico, and a Mexican government that uses illegal immigration to the U.S. as (in the words of former foreign minister Jorge Castañeda) a "safety valve." But there are literally billions of people willing to work for even less than Mexicans are. "In this age of cheap jet travel, poor Mexican immigrant job hunters might find themselves undercut by even poorer temporary workers from, say, Bangladesh who may be willing to work for even less," Sailer predicts. "According to UN figures, there are several billion people poorer than the average Mexican."

With hi-tech and manufacturing jobs fleeing the country, and millions of low-skill workers flooding in, what will America look like just a few years from now if Bush's amnesty proposal is enacted?

Consolidating the Continent

The January 8 *New York Times* editorially praised the Bush amnesty as a prelude to a larger effort to reform our immigration system: "For simply reopening what has always been a torturous debate in this country, the president deserves applause. He has recognized that the nation's immigration system is, as he put it, 'broken.'" But the unspoken purpose of the process the Bush plan would inaugurate is to demolish, rather than repair, what remains of our immigration system.

The invited audience for President Bush's January 7 White House announcement included representatives from various "citizen groups," such as the Hispanic Alliance for Progress, the Association for the Advancement of Mexican Americans, the Latino Coalition, and the League of United Latin American Citizens. The address itself served as an overture for a hastily called "Summit of the Americas" in Monterrey, Mexico, the following week. These two facts underscore the real purpose of the amnesty proposal: It is a significant step toward the amalgamation of the U.S. with Mexico—as well as Canada, and eventually every other country in this hemisphere—into a regional political bloc.

Shortly after taking office, Mr. Bush and Mexican President Vicente Fox signed a document called the "Guanajuato Proposal," pledging that their governments would "strive to consolidate a North American economic community whose benefits reach the lesser-developed areas of the region and extend to the most vulnerable social groups in our countries."

Within a few months of that declaration, the Mexican government had composed a five-point program to hasten "consolidation" with the U.S.:

- Legalization of "undocumented" workers (that is, illegal aliens from Mexico);
- An expanded permanent visas program;
- An enhanced guest workers visas program;
- Border control cooperation;
- Economic development in immigrant-sending regions of Mexico.

This list of demands, according to then-Mexican Foreign Minister Jorge Castañeda, were essentially non-negotiable: He insisted that the U.S. had to accept "the whole enchilada, or nothing." The Bush administration has dutifully worked to meet that nation's demands without exacting anything from Mexico in return.

The U.S.-Mexico Agenda

During Fox's 2001 visit to the U.S., the groundwork was laid for the so-called "Partnership for Prosperity" (PfP)—an initiative designed to use American tax dollars to build Mexico's manufacturing sector. According to the U.S. State Department, PfP's action plan calls for U.S. assistance— meaning taxpayer subsidies—to Mexico to boost investment in housing and commercial infrastructure to boost Mexican productivity. This has the unavoidable effect of drawing manufacturing jobs south of the border—even as low-wage jobs are increasingly snapped up by illegal immigrants (pardon me—future temporary workers) surging northward.

The Bush administration's indecent eagerness to eradicate our southern border and consolidate our nation with Mexico was noted by *Newsweek* political analyst Howard Fineman. "Whatever else George W. Bush does, or doesn't do, he has earned a place in history as the first American president to place Hispanic voters at the center of politics, and the first to view the land between Canada and Guatemala as one," noted Fineman. "It makes sense, if you think about it: Texas, long ago and far away, was part of Mexico. Now a Texan is trying to reassemble the Old Country, and then some."

"The ultimate goal of any White House policy ought to be a North American economic and political alliance similar in scope and ambition to the European Union," opined an *Atlanta Journal-Constitution* editorial on September 7, 2001. "Unlike the varied landscapes and cultures of European Union members, the United States, Canada and Mexico already share a great deal in common, and language is not as great a barrier. President Bush, for example, is quite comfortable with the blended Mexican-Anglo culture forged in the border states of Texas, California and Arizona."

President Bush has only offered oblique hints of the agenda that Fineman correctly described. Mexican President Fox has been more candid.

During a May 16, 2002 speech in Madrid, Fox boasted: "In the last few months we have managed to achieve an improvement in the situation of many Mexicans in [the United States], regardless of their migratory status, through schemes that have permitted them access to health and education systems, identity documents, as well as the full respect for their human rights." Here Fox referred to the incremental legalization illegal Mexican immigrants achieved when various state and local governments began to accept matricula consular cards as official ID. Those cards are issued by Mexican consulates without regard to the recipient's legal status. Easily counterfeited, the matricula cards give illegal aliens access to employment, health benefits, banking services and—in some states—driver's licenses.

In the Madrid speech, Fox explained that demolishing the distinction between legal and illegal Mexican immigrants is necessary in order to advance the merger of the U.S. and Mexico: "Eventually our long-range objective is to establish

with the United States, but also with Canada, our other regional partner, an ensemble of connections and institutions
similar to those created by the European Union, with the
goal of attending to future themes [such as] the future prosperity of North America, and the movement of capital,
goods, services, and persons." Such movement of persons
would no longer be "immigration" or "emigration"—terms
referring to the crossing of international borders—but
merely "migration" within one vast political entity. In other
words: goodbye to U.S. citizenship.

Significantly, in his remarks at the January 12 press conference in Monterrey, Fox pointedly, and repeatedly, used
the term "migration" to refer to the Bush plan, referring
variously to "that migration topic," "the migration matters," "this migration proposal," the "migration flow," and
so on. Tellingly, he also referred to "the leaders of the countries of America"—rather than to national leaders of separate and independent nations.

Betraying America's Borders

Amnesty for illegal aliens, a central piece in the agenda for
hemispheric consolidation, would almost certainly have
been announced long ago were it not for 9-11—an event
that demonstrated, in a tragic and lethal fashion, the mor-
tal danger resulting from the failure to secure our borders.

However, merger-minded elites in both the U.S. and Mexico regrouped and continued their campaign for amnesty.
Last fall, a coalition of radical groups—including the Communist Party—organized the "Immigrant Workers Freedom
Ride." In that campaign, busloads of illegal aliens were
brought to Washington to lobby on behalf of amnesty.

Vicente Fox did his part by visiting three southwestern
states—Texas, Arizona and New Mexico—to lobby state
legislatures to support the amnesty drive. "We share nation
and language," Fox told the New Mexico legislature. "In addition to our geographical vicinity, we are united by inseparable bonds, history, values and interests. . . . We must

join together. . . . You need Mexico and Mexicans, and we need you."

Acting as the supposed leader of "Mexicans living abroad" (a group that, according to the Mexican government, includes Americans of Mexican ancestry born in this country), Fox demanded that lawmakers in this country "facilitate access to health care and education services for all those who share our border. . . . Without this, it is impossible to think about the path to greater integration and shared prosperity."

Open borders, amnesty for illegals, subsidies for Mexico's economy, exporting manufacturing capacity south of the border, expanded welfare benefits for foreigners who entered our nation illegally—these are all part of the same seamless design. As Fox himself put it, that design is the "integration" of the U.S. and Mexico into a hemisphere-wide political unit.

Many observers believe that the Bush amnesty plan is part of a political strategy aimed at courting the Hispanic vote—which would be a shockingly cynical and opportunistic venture. But the truth is even worse: President Bush is consciously betraying our nation by undermining our borders, our sovereignty, and the integrity of our laws. And he is doing this as part of a campaign that will—if successful—result in an end to our national independence and our constitutional order.

Every American worthy of the name must not accept this incredible betrayal—and must not allow it to be consummated.

1790

The first U.S. government census reveals that forty-four thousand Irish immigrants live in the United States. The Naturalization Act of 1790 grants the right of U.S. citizenship to all "free white persons."

1795

The Naturalization Act of 1795 restricts American citizenship to "free white persons" who have resided in the United States for five years and have renounced allegiance to their native country.

1798

The Naturalization Act is revised again, with a fourteen-year residency requirement established. Under the Alien and Sedition Acts, the president can deport any foreigner he deems dangerous.

1830

The first major wave of immigrants, primarily from western and northern Europe, begins to arrive in the United States; over 7 million will arrive in the next fifty years.

1843

The American Republican Party is formed in New York. Known unofficially as the Know-Nothing Party, its followers are staunch opponents of immigration.

1845–1847

The Irish potato famine sparks massive emigration from Ireland.

1848

The Treaty of Guadalupe Hidalgo is signed, ending the Mexican-American War. Mexico agrees to give the United States territory that includes modern-day Texas, California, Nevada, and Utah, along with portions of New Mexico, Arizona, Wyoming, and Colorado. The treaty also awards U.S. citizenship to approximately eighty thousand former Mexican residents.

1849

The California gold rush spurs emigration from China.

1854

Candidates from the Know-Nothing Party capture every statewide office in Massachusetts and win local elections in several other states.

1864

Congress passes the Act to Encourage Immigration, also known as the Contract Labor Law. The act is the first federal immigration law; it creates the Bureau of Immigration, bars criminals and prostitutes from entering the country, and makes pre-emigration contracts binding.

1868

The Fourteenth Amendment to the Constitution is ratified, guaranteeing American citizenship to anyone born on U.S. soil. The Burlingame Treaty between the United States and China permits Chinese immigration but bars Chinese from becoming naturalized citizens.

1870

The Naturalization Act of 1870 bars Asians from U.S. citizenship, limiting citizenship to "white persons and persons of African descent."

1880

The second major wave of immigration begins, with most of the new arrivals coming from southern and eastern Europe.

1882

The Exclusion Act of 1882 suspends immigration from China for ten years and bars the immigration of convicts and the insane. The act is made permanent in 1902.

1891

Congress passes an act that makes polygamists, "persons suffering from a loathsome or a dangerous contagious disease," and those convicted of "a misdemeanor involving moral turpitude" ineligible for immigration. The act also establishes the Bureau of Immigration.

1892

Ellis Island opens; 12 million immigrants are processed there over the next thirty years.

1901

The assassination of President William McKinley by anarchist Leon Czolgosz prompts Congress to enact the Anarchist Exclusion Act, which allows immigrants to be barred from entering the United States on the basis of their political opinions.

1907

The Expatriation Act states that an American woman who marries a foreign national loses her citizenship. The Immigration Act of 1907 bars the immigration of "imbeciles, feeble-minded persons, unaccompanied children under seventeen years of age, and persons who are found to be and are certified by the examination surgeon as being mentally or physically defective." The Gentleman's Agreement between the governments of the United States and Japan stops Japanese immigration, with the exception of the wives and fiancées of Japanese men who are already living in the United States.

1917

The Immigration Act of 1917 prohibits immigration from Asia, with the exception of Japan and the Philippines and requires immigrants to pass literacy tests in order to enter the United States.

1921

Congress passes the Quota Act of 1921, which reduces the number of immigrants admitted to the United States and establishes a quota system based on the 1910 census. Affecting only European immigration, it restricts annual immigration to 3 percent of the number of a nationality group living in the United States as of 1910.

1922

The Cable Act partially repeals the Expatriation Act, but under the new act an American woman who marries an Asian national still loses her U.S. citizenship.

1923

The Supreme Court rules in *U.S. v. Bhaghat Singh Thind* that Asian Indians could not become naturalized U.S. citizens.

1924

The Johnson-Reed Act, also known as the National Origin Act of 1924, is enacted. It revises the 1921 act by relying on the census figures of 1890 and limiting annual European immigration to 2 percent of the number of the nationality group. The Oriental Exclusion Act bans most immigration from Asia.

1933

The Immigration and Naturalization Service (INS) is created.

1940

The Alien Registration Act requires the registration and fingerprinting of all noncitizens over the age of fourteen.

1942

Needing manual labor because of World War II, the U.S. and Mexican governments initiate the Bracero program. Approximately 300,000 to 350,000 poor Mexican workers are allowed to enter the United States each year.

1943

The Exclusion Act is repealed and a quota is established for Chinese immigration.

1946

The Luce-Cellar Act allows Filipinos and Asian Indians to become U.S. citizens.

1948

The Displaced Persons Act allows Europeans who had become refugees after World War II to immigrate to the United States outside of the 1924 quotas. In addition, Chinese residents who had been trapped in the United States due to China's civil war are allowed to remain in the United States and are given permanent resident status.

1950

The Internal Security Act prohibits foreign Communists from entering the United States.

1952

The McCarran-Walter Immigration Act reaffirms the 1924 quota and limits total annual immigration to one-sixth of 1 percent of the population of the continental United States in 1920; exceptions are made for the spouses and children of U.S. citizens and for people born in the Western Hemisphere.

1954

The rise of illegal Mexican immigration into Texas and California prompts the U.S. government to establish Operation Wetback. Illegal immigrants are rounded up and sent back to Mexico.

1964

The Bracero program officially ends.

1965

The Immigration Act of 1965 is enacted, ending forty years of national quotas. The federal government replaces that with a worldwide quota; regardless of its population, each country can contribute an equal number of immigrants, based on the worldwide number.

1968

The third major wave of immigration into the United States begins.

1986

The Immigration Reform and Control Act of 1986 offers amnesty to all illegal immigrants in the United States at that time.

1990

Congress passes Immigration Act of 1990. The act increases the worldwide quota and creates an immigration lottery.

1996

The Illegal Immigration Reform and Immigrant Responsibility Act makes it more difficult for refugees to gain asylum and strengthens border enforcement.

2003

The INS is dissolved and all its responsibilities are shifted to the Department of Homeland Security.

Organizations to Contact

The editors have compiled the following list of organizations concerned with the topics contained in this book. The descriptions are derived from materials provided by the organizations. All have publications or information available for interested readers. The list was compiled on the date of publication of the present volume; the information provided here may change. Be aware that many organizations take several weeks or longer to respond to inquiries, so allow as much time as possible.

American Immigration Control Foundation

PO Box 525, Monterey, VA 24465
(540) 468-2022 • fax: (540) 468-2024
e-mail: aicfndn@cfw.com • Web site: www.aicfoundation.com

The American Immigration Control Foundation is an independent research and education organization that believes massive immigration, especially illegal immigration, is harming America. It calls for an end to illegal immigration and for stricter controls on legal immigration. The foundation publishes several pamphlets, monographs, and booklets, including *Selling Our Birthright, Huddled Cliches*, and *Erasing America: The Politics of the Borderless Nation*.

American Immigration Law Foundation (AILF)

918 F St. NW, 6th Fl., Washington, DC 20004
(202) 742-5600 • fax: (202) 742-5619
e-mail: info@ailf.org • Web site: www.ailf.org

The American Immigration Law Foundation is an educational and charitable organization that seeks to increase public understanding of immigration law and of the contributions of immigrants to American society. The AILF has four core program areas: the Legal Action Center, the Immigration Policy Center, the Public Education Program, and the Exchange Visitor Program. Policy briefs, reports, and commentaries are available on the Web site. In addition, the *Immigration Policy Focus*, which is published several times each year, provides analyses of immigration issues.

Americans for Immigration Control (AIC)
PO Box 738, Monterey, VA 24465
(540) 468-2023 • fax: (540) 468-2026
e-mail: aic@immigrationcontrol.com
Web site: www.immigrationcontrol.com

AIC is a lobbying organization that works to influence Congress to adopt legal reforms that would reduce U.S. immigration. It calls for increased funding for the U.S. Border Patrol and the deployment of military forces to prevent illegal immigration. It also supports sanctions against employers who hire illegal immigrants and opposes amnesty for such immigrants. AIC offers articles and brochures that state its position on immigration.

California Coalition for Immigration Reform (CCIR)
PO Box 2744-117, Huntington Beach, CA 92649
(714) 665-2500 • (714) 846-9682 • fax: (714) 846-9682
e-mail: barb@ccir.net • Web site: www.ccir.net

CCIR is a grassroots volunteer organization representing Americans concerned with illegal immigration. It seeks to educate and inform the public and to effectively ensure enforcement of the nation's immigration laws. CCIR publishes alerts, bulletins, videotapes, and audiotapes, some of which are available on its Web site.

Center for Immigration Studies
1522 K St. NW, Suite 820, Washington, DC 20005-1202
(202) 466-8185 • fax: (202) 466-8076
e-mail: center@cis.org • Web site: www.cis.org

The center studies the effects of immigration on the economic, social, demographic, and environmental conditions in the United States. It believes that the large number of recent immigrants has become a burden on America and favors reforming immigration laws to make them more consistent with U.S. interests. The center publishes editorials, reports, and position papers, such as "Immigration and American Workers: Study Examines Impact of Immigration on Wages."

El Rescate
1313 West Eighth St., Suite 200, Los Angeles, CA 90017
(213) 387-3284 • fax: (213) 387-9189
Web site: www.elrescate.org

El Rescate provides free legal and social services to Central American refugees. It is involved in federal litigation to uphold the constitutional rights of refugees and illegal immigrants. It compiles and distributes articles and information and publishes the newsletter *El Rescate*.

Federation for American Immigration Reform (FAIR)
1666 Connecticut Ave. NW, Suite 400, Washington, DC 20009
(202) 328-7004 • fax: (202) 387-3447
e-mail: comments@fairus.org • Web site: www.fairus.org

FAIR works to stop illegal immigration and to limit legal immigration. It believes that the growing flood of immigrants into the United States causes higher unemployment and taxes social services. FAIR publishes a monthly newsletter, reports, and position papers, including *Running in Place: Immigration and U.S. Energy Usage*.

National Council of La Raza (NCLR)
1111 Nineteenth St. NW, Suite 1000, Washington, DC 20036
(202) 785-1670
Web site: www.nclr.org

NCLR is a national organization that seeks to improve opportunities for Americans of Hispanic descent. It conducts research on many issues, including immigration, and opposes restrictive immigration laws. The council publishes and distributes congressional testimony and policy reports, including *Unfinished Business: The Immigration Control and Reform Act of 1986* and *Unlocking the Golden Door: Hispanics and the Citizenship Process*.

National Immigration Forum
50 F St. NW, Suite 300, Washington, DC 20001
(202) 347-0047
e-mail: info@immigrationforum.org
Web site: www.immigrationforum.org

The forum believes that immigration strengthens America and that welfare benefits do not attract illegal immigrants. It supports effective measures aimed at curbing illegal immigration and promotes programs and policies that help refugees and immigrants assimilate into American society. The forum publishes the annual *Immigration Policy Handbook* as well as editorials, press releases, and fact sheets, many of which are available on the Web site.

National Network for Immigrant and Refugee Rights
310 Eighth St., Suite 303, Oakland, CA 94607
(510) 465-1984 • fax: (510) 465-1885
e-mail: nnirr@nnirr.org • Web site: www.nnirr.org

The network includes community, church, labor, and legal groups committed to the cause of equal rights for all immigrants. These groups work to end discrimination and unfair treatment of illegal immigrants and refugees. The network aims to strengthen and coordinate educational efforts among immigration advocates nationwide. It publishes reports, including *From the Borderline to the Colorline: A Report on Anti-Immigrant Racism in the United States*, and a monthly newsletter, *Network News*.

Negative Population Growth, Inc. (NPG)
2861 Duke St., Suite 36, Alexandria, VA 22314
(703) 370-9510 • fax: (703) 370-9514
e-mail: npg@npg.org • Web site: www.npg.org

NPG believes that world population must be reduced and that the United States is already overpopulated. It calls for an end to illegal immigration and an annual cap on legal immigration of 200,000 people in order to achieve "zero net migration." The organization publishes position papers on population and immigration in its *NPG Forum*, as well as a quarterly newsletter, *Population and Resource Outlook*.

NumbersUSA.com
1601 N. Kent St., Suite 1100, Arlington, VA 22209
(703) 816-8820
e-mail: info@numbersusa.com

NumbersUSA.com is a nonpartisan public policy organization that aims to reduce the overall levels of immigration in order to achieve an environmentally sustainable and economically just United States. News articles, congressional testimony, and studies on immigration are among the materials available on the site.

U.S. Citizenship and Immigration Service (USCIS)
U.S. Department of Homeland Security, Washington, DC 20528
Web site: www.uscis.gov

The USCIS, an agency of the Department of Homeland Defense, is charged with administrative and management functions and responsibilities that were once in the former Immigration and Naturalization Service, including the enforcing immigration laws and regulations, as well as administering immigrant-related services. It produces numerous reports and evaluations on selected programs.

U.S. Committee for Refugees and Immigrants
1717 Massachusetts Ave. NW, 2nd Fl.
Washington, DC 20036-2003
(202) 347-3507 • fax: (202) 347-3418
Web site: www.refugeesusa.org

The U.S. Committee for Refugees and Immigrants is an organization that addresses the rights of immigrants and refugees throughout the world by promoting humane public policy and providing professional services to migrants. Its publications include the annual *World Refugee Survey* and the journal *Refugee Reports*.

Web Site

Digital History: Guided Readings: The Huddled Masses, www. digitalhistory.uh.edu/database/subtitles.cfm?TitleID=59.

This page, which is part of the Digital History Web site, provides information on a number of issues relating to the past and modern immigration, such as its effects on the U.S. economy, migration and disease, and immigration restriction. The Web site is a collaboration between the University of Houston, Chicago Historical Society, Gilder Lehrman Institute of American History, the Museum of Fine Arts in Houston, the National Park Service, and the Project for the Active Teaching of American History (PATH).

Roy Beck, *The Case Against Immigration: The Moral, Economic, Social, and Environmental Reasons for Reducing U.S. immigration Back to Traditional Levels.* New York: W.W. Norton, 1996.

John Bodnar, *The Transplanted: A History of Immigrants in Urban America.* Bloomington: Indiana University Press, 1985.

David Cole, *Enemy Aliens: Double Standards and Constitutional Freedoms in the War on Terrorism.* New York: New Press, 2003.

Roger Daniels, *Guarding the Golden Door: American Immigration Policy and Immigrants Since 1882.* New York: Hill and Wang, 2004.

LeeAnne Gelletly, *Mexican Immigration.* Philadelphia: Mason Crest, 2004.

Edward Hutchinson, *Immigrants and Their Children, 1850–1950.* New York: Wiley, 1956.

Tamar Jacoby, ed., *Reinventing the Melting Pot: The New Immigrants and What It Means to Be American.* New York: Basic Books, 2003.

Susanne Jonas and Suzie Dod Thomas, eds., *Immigration: A Civil Rights Issue for the Americas.* Wilmington, DE: Scholarly Resources, 1999.

Abraham J. Karp, ed., *Golden Door to America: The Jewish Immigrant Experience.* New York: Viking Press, 1976.

Philip Kayal and Adele L. Younis, eds., *The Coming of the Arabic-Speaking People to the United States.* Staten Island, NY: Center for Migration Studies, 1995.

Kevin Kenny, *The American Irish: A History.* New York: Pearson Education Limited, 2000.

Dale T. Knobel, *"America for the Americans": The Nativist Movement in the United States.* New York: Twayne, 1996.

Alan Kraut, *Silent Travelers: Germs, Genes, and the "Immigrant Menace."* New York: BasicBooks, 1994.

Gerald Leinwand, *American Immigration: Should the Open Door Be Closed?* New York: F. Watts, 1995.

Michelle Malkin, *Invasion: How America Still Welcomes Terrorists, Criminals, and Other Foreign Menaces to Our Shores.* Washington, DC: Regnery, 2002.

Kerby Miller and Paul Wagner, *Out of Ireland: The Story of Irish Emigration to America.* Washington, DC: Elliott & Clark, 1994.

Joel Millman, *The Other Americans: How Immigrants Renew Our Country, Our Economy, and Our Values.* New York: Viking, 1997.

Joseph Nevins, *Operation Gatekeeper: The Rise of the "Illegal Alien" and the Remaking of the U.S.-Mexico Boundary.* New York: Routledge, 2002.

David M. Reimers, *Unwelcome Strangers: American Identity and the Turn Against Immigration.* New York: Columbia University Press, 1998.

John Tenhula, *Voices from Southeast Asia: The Refugee Experience in the United States.* New York: Holmes & Meier, 1991.

Harry Shih-Shan Tsai, *The Chinese Experience in America.* Bloomington: Indiana University Press, 1986.

Chilton Williamson, *The Immigration Mystique: America's False Conscience.* New York: BasicBooks, 1996.

Index

Operation Wetback of, 181–85
power of, 188–89
reclassification of offenses by,
192–94
Immigration Reform and Control
Act, 22
INS. *See* Immigration and
Naturalization Service
Irish Americans, 16, 19, 29–33
Irish immigrants
are threat to American politics,
29–33
prejudice against, 13–16
Italian immigrants, 154

Jackson, Sheila, 192
Japanese immigrants, 19–20
Japanese internment camps, 20,
41–48
Jewish immigrants
nativist sentiment against,
16–19
quotas targeting, 153–54
U.S. should have responded
better to, 104–12
job protection, limited
immigration for, 132–33
see also U.S. labor force
John Birch Society, 22
John Paul II (pope), 76–77
Johnson-Reed Act. *See*
Immigration Act, of 1924

Karp, Abraham J., 17
Kenny, Kevin, 14, 16, 19
Kensington riots, 14
Kneeland, Douglas E., 123
Know-Nothing Party, 15, 153
Kraus, Alan M., 27

labor force. *See* U.S. labor force
Latin Americans, 59–60
Lee, Jackson, 192
legislation
against illegal immigrants, is too

harsh, 186–94
limiting immigration, 20
is misguided, 95–103
see also specific legislation
Limbaugh, Rush, 51

Madison, James, 31
Malkin, Michelle, 69
Malvo, Lee, 71
mandatory detention, 191–92
marriage rights, 130–35
Massachusetts, anti-immigration
sentiment in, 15
McCarran-Walter Immigration
Act. *See* Immigration and
Nationality Act of 1952
McCarthy, Joseph, 158
McCollum, Bill, 192
Meissner, Doris, 188–89
Mercurio (ship), 184–85
Mexican immigrants
bracero program and, 20–21,
181–85
debate over, 20–22
illegal, 73–75
influence of, 59–60
Operation Wetback and,
181–85
racial identity of, 140–41
temporary worker program
and, 212–21
Monk, Maria, 15
Muhammad, John, 71
multiculturalism
benefits America, 58–62
harms America, 49–57
Muslim immigrants, 22–23

nationality, meaning of, 142–44
national origins, invention of,
141–50
national security
immigrants threaten, 69–77,
92–93
refugee policies and, 80